Down to Earth

DOWN TO EARTH:
The Hopes & Fears of All the Years
Are Met in Thee Tonight

Down to Earth
978-1-5018-2339-8
978-1-5018-2340-4 eBook
978-1-5018-2341-1 Large Print

Down to Earth: Devotions for the Season
978-1-5018-2344-2
978-1-5018-2345-9 eBook

Down to Earth: DVD
978-1-5018-2346-6

Down to Earth: Leader Guide
978-1-5018-2342-8
978-1-5018-2343-5 eBook

Down to Earth: Youth Study Book
978-1-5018-2352-7
978-1-5018-2353-4 eBook

Down to Earth: Children's Leader Guide
978-1-5018-2354-1

Also by Mike Slaughter

Change the World
Christmas Is Not Your Birthday
Dare to Dream
Hijacked
Momentum for Life
Money Matters
Real Followers
Renegade Gospel

shiny gods
Spiritual Entrepreneurs
The Christian Wallet
The Passionate Church
UnLearning Church
Upside Living in a
    Downside Economy

For more information, visit www.MikeSlaughter.com.

Mike Slaughter

The
Hopes & Fears
of All the Years

Down
TO
Earth

Are Met in
Thee
Tonight

With
Rachel Billups

Abingdon Press / Nashville

DOWN TO EARTH
The Hopes and Fears of All the Years Are Met in Thee Tonight

This book is printed on elemental chlorine-free paper.

Library of Congress Cataloging-in-Publication data applied for.

978-1-5018-2339-8

16 17 18 19 20 21 22 23 24 25—10 9 8 7 6 5 4 3 2 1
MANUFACTURED IN THE UNITED STATES OF AMERICA

Mike
Dedicated to our grandson Jack Brian Slaughter
on his first Christmas

Rachel
To my mom and dad, Paul and Linda Fast,
and their faithful service to Jesus

Contents

Introduction

Introduction

Mike

The Word became flesh and blood,
and moved into the neighborhood.
(John 1:14 The Message)

Advent is a season of anticipation. The focus extends far beyond the hyped marketing glitz that serves as a siren call to the lures of consumerist idolatry. Advent is the expectation that Jesus will come in the present to birth in us God's new work. It is a season of active preparation as we welcome Jesus down to earth.

Many have considered Jesus' resurrection from the grave—an event that forever changed the trajectory of human history—as the greatest and most powerful miracle of all time. It's true that without the Resurrection, Jesus could not have been the Christ. Rightful repayment would not have been made for the transgressions of humanity throughout time, including yours and mine.

Yet, to me the Resurrection is not the greatest of God's miracles, nor even the most unique. After all, Scripture includes numerous "raisings from the dead": Elijah resurrected the son of Zarephath's widow; Elisha resurrected the son of the great Shunammite woman; and Jesus resurrected Jairus's daughter, the widow's son at Nain, and, of course, Lazarus.

I believe the greatest miracle of all time was Jesus' birth: God Almighty willingly choosing to become God incarnate, God in the flesh. The Lord of the Universe, as a vulnerable babe, entered into the struggles of humankind at a tumultuous time and in a nondescript place. The God of heaven "made himself nothing by taking the very nature of a servant, being made in human likeness" (Philippians 2:7), and in so doing chose willingly to humble himself as a "down-to-earth" God.

Frankly, if God had chosen to be just "Our Father who art in heaven," if we had never experienced God with skin on in the person of Jesus, then God might always have remained an ethereal concept.

To those who have never met Jesus, even today God can seem like a distant paternal image, emanating only a faint and benign love that feels more dutiful than authentic. Even worse, God can appear to be a harsh, mercurial, authoritarian figure who metes out rewards or punishments at will. This latter concept of God more closely resembles the pantheon of petulant, unreliable, and all-too-human gods of ancient Rome and Greece—sometimes kind but more often cruel and unpredictable. The relationship between the people and these so-called gods was much more about appeasement than about loving intimacy.

Encountering a God who looks and acts like Jesus is an entirely different proposition. In Jesus, we have the picture of a God who intentionally positions himself as a mere servant, identifying with the lowest of lows, the least, and the lost. As the Son of God, Jesus is the antithesis of the spoiled, prideful, and cruelly powerful prince of Greek mythology or fairy-tale lore who willfully acts on personal whims for selfish gain. Instead Jesus, the down-to-earth God, demonstrates in the flesh and to the full the love, humility, obedience, and sacrificial lifestyle that we as Jesus' followers are in turn called to live out and embrace.

Christmas each year is the best reminder I know that God loved us so much that he willingly emptied himself of all divine rights and privileges, sacrificing everything so that we as God's children might have everything.

In the chapters ahead, Pastor Rachel Billups and I will explore this down-to-earth God who walks, talks, lives, and loves like Jesus. We will explore what Jesus' love and transforming power can mean in our lives and the lives of others, as we act on Jesus' directives to love our neighbors as ourselves, welcome the stranger, reach the lost, and set the oppressed free.

Many of us right now may be struggling to feel any sense of Advent anticipation. Perhaps this Advent you have just gone through the pain of divorce. You may be experiencing the devastating effects of betrayal and broken trust. You could be in the midst of a transition in employment because of company downsizing. Maybe the doctor has informed you about the result of a biopsy, and it has sabotaged your hope and shredded your faith.

Take heart! Immanuel, God with us, is about to birth a new thing in you and through you. As the prophet Isaiah declared, God is "making a way in the wilderness and streams in the wasteland" (Isaiah 43:19). In the pages ahead, we will explore together what it means to comprehend and embrace the down-to-earth God we serve.

1.
Down to Earth
Love

1.

Down to Earth Love

Rachel

Therefore if you have any encouragement from being united with Christ, if any comfort from his love, if any common sharing in the Spirit, if any tenderness and compassion, then make my joy complete by being like-minded, having the same love, being one in spirit and of one mind.
(Philippians 2:1-2)

Thanksgiving at the Billups' household is an adventure. It's not unusual for us to be gathered with in-laws and out-laws, strangers and friends. With such a diverse group, conversation can get interesting. Because of a deep desire to enjoy our meal, I tend to steer the conversation away from anything that would create an argument—no political banter, zero comments about the current presidential administration, no discussion around the plight of refugees throughout the world, and we promise to refrain from talking about those not present. However, my efforts are not always successful.

Perhaps your family gatherings are not as conversationally exhausting as ours. Even at our house, though, in the midst of all the verbal gymnastics, one thing brings unity, one secret weapon of love: my mother's pie. Nobody argues about my mother's pie—it is her spiritual gift. The pie is always delicious, always baked to perfection. When the conversation gets to the point of no return, I speak these magic words, "Who wants pie?" and suddenly love fills the air. If only we lived in a world where we could negotiate all conflicts with pie.

PIES, NOT CUPS

I would like to believe that the church is that world. Perhaps you know some folk in your church who use food to negotiate conflicts. That could be the original purpose for the potluck dinner. But when I peer among the four walls of the church, I see the same conversational gymnastics or, worse, the disunity created by argument and debate. Unity may be a clear marker of the church we read about in the New Testament, but it appears that churches in the United States are so concerned with being right, with winning an argument, that the simplest of controversies can send us over the edge. And it would seem there is not enough pie in the world to fix it.

About a year ago my husband, Jon, the kids, and I were waiting outside a movie theater to watch *Inside Out*. As we waited, we did what every red-blooded American family does when waiting—we played on our smartphones. I was scrolling through Facebook when I noticed that my feed was bombarded with posts about Starbucks and its new red cup. According to some comments, the cup's new design was a slam on Christianity and how we, as followers of Jesus, celebrate Christmas.[1]

I was confused and frustrated. I could feel the cynicism rising up inside of me. Questions began to pour out: "Is this real? What do snowflakes and reindeer even have to do with Jesus?" "Why are we arguing about something as silly as a red cup?" I wanted to set someone straight, to shout out loud, "Is Starbucks even a Christian company?" But I did not respond—and I did not need to, because plenty of folk responded for me. There were arguments for the red cup, against the red cup, and even those who criticized people on both sides.

Could it have been a flash-marketing scheme driven by Starbucks itself? Yes, but even if it was, we fell for it. Why? Because we love to be right. Followers of Jesus are capable of having some pretty heated debates with anyone and everyone who is willing to listen. I am all for a passionate conversation, but is that really what we are engaging in? Or in arguing about things such as red cups, sexual identity issues, who we voted for, and where refugees should go, are we allowing these issues to create dividing lines between us?

These divisions, these arguments, present a devilish distraction. When we think of each other as the enemy and talk at each other with hate, evil wins. At best these arguments present a distraction, and at worst they actually tear us apart. We allow our differences—theological and practical—to tear down the body of Christ.

I believe the world isn't looking for more hate that divides; it is looking for love (that delicious pie) that is approachable and accessible, love that lives right where we are, love that comes right down to earth.

In This Together

I do not know why you are interested in Christianity. You could be reading this book for all kinds of reasons. Perhaps you have grown up in the church your whole life. Perhaps you have been driven to faith in Jesus because of the guilt of bad choices. Maybe you have welcomed children into your household and believe you could use some holy help. Whatever the reason, we as followers of Jesus are in this together. We are following a Jesus who was messy when love came down to earth. Jesus spent his time with religious folk and nonreligious folk, saints and sinners. He loved people who were hard to love. Jesus sacrificed his life for the whole lump of them, for all of us. We are in this together.

At Advent, we step together into a season in the life of the church that is as terrifying and beautiful as waiting for your child to be born. Advent is a spiritual gestation—waiting, preparing, anticipating, at the same time knowing that right here, right now there is life—*real* life—growing inside of us. We aren't just waiting for an event; we are experiencing a spiritual awakening that has changed, can change, and will change the world forever. I am not asking any of us to pretend we understand everything there is to know about this faith we call Christianity, or to cover up the fact that people who follow Jesus do not always respond to life's challenges and other Jesus followers in civil ways. But Advent is a "down-to-earth" invitation to do a heart check and ask ourselves, "How can I discover and explore what it means to be a down-to-earth people? How can I live Jesus' down-to-earth kind of love?"

Advent is a spiritual gestation— waiting, preparing, anticipating, at the same time knowing that right here, right now there is life—*real* life— growing inside of us.

When we open the pages of the New Testament, we realize that even the first followers of Jesus argued about red cups. Okay, maybe it wasn't red cups, but early Christians did argue about whether the inside or outside of the cup needed to be clean, when to wash their hands, and whether people were made for the Sabbath or the Sabbath was made for people. They also created dividing lines among themselves. This is not a new temptation or struggle. But in Scripture, we are afforded a glimpse of Jesus' down-to-earth kind of love.

One of the most profound pictures of that love is found in Paul's letter to the Philippians. Philippians is not typically a book of the Bible that churches talk about during Advent and Christmas, but it works well here because this Scripture is all about Jesus coming down to earth. Paul was writing from prison to a group of Jesus followers in Philippi. The followers seemed to have a deep relationship with Paul. Earlier, it had been Paul who had helped this group say yes to following Jesus.

As we read through the letter, we discover that Paul was deeply concerned about how this fledging group of Jesus followers was faring. It seems that they had allowed arguments and differences to divide them, and Paul didn't want that to happen. So he wrote them a letter. Philippians 2 is a beautiful hymn prefaced by these words:

> Therefore if you have any encouragement from being united with Christ, if any comfort from his love, if any common sharing in the Spirit, if any tenderness and compassion, then make my joy complete by being like-minded, having the same love, being one in spirit and of one mind. Do nothing out of selfish ambition or vain conceit. Rather, in humility value others above yourselves, not looking to your own interests but each of you to the interests of the others.
>
> (Philippians 2:1-4)

Paul was asking the followers at Philippi, and is asking us, a really tough question: *Has following Jesus made a difference in your life?* On the surface this may seem like a personal question, as though it's about my relationship with Jesus. But in fact the form of *you* used in the first sentence is plural, meaning "all of you." Paul was writing to the community as a whole.

Sometimes it is difficult for followers of Jesus in our individualistic culture to realize that following Jesus is not merely about Jesus and me. Faith in Jesus is not about *my* ambitions, *my* opinions, *my* interests, or even *our* differences, *our* arguments, or *our* desire to be right. Faith is not about just me or my relationship with you; faith is demonstrated in us! Following Jesus is about what we do together and how we treat one another—both those who are part of the body of Christ and those who are not.

NOT ABOUT US

I am part of a faith community that reminds itself that following Jesus is a team sport. It's not all about me, and it's not even about us. Christmas is not your birthday! When we use that phrase, we are referring to the trend during the holiday season for folk to spend money they do not have, sometimes buying things that recipients do not need, often for people we don't even like. In 2015, adults in the U.S planned to spend $830 on Christmas, a ninety-dollar increase from the year before.[2] And though there were shops that closed on Thanksgiving and stores that participated in the #OPTOUT campaign against Black Friday, it's still the time of the year when we participate in a spending frenzy. Even followers of Jesus bless our desire for more stuff with the excuse, "'Tis the season."

I like stuff as much as anyone else, but I believe we can't and won't find our value, our worth, in what we buy. We start to believe the fallacy, "If only I could have this, then I would be happy." Or worse, "If only I could get my kids or grandkids this, then they would love me."

If we don't spend ourselves into debt or allow ourselves to be lured into purchasing more than we need, we can still fall into the trap of focusing on ourselves by treating what we do for Jesus as a badge of honor. Our acts or gifts of service can become more about acquiring accolades than remembering the love-filled privilege it is to participate in God's work.

Most of us can remember moments in our journey with Jesus when we do things because they will get us something—make us more important to our church, to our family, and maybe even to God. It's a form of control, and it's really just another way of getting what we want.

As a mother and daughter, I struggle with this one. When I am hosting a holiday gathering, I want people to feel loved and welcomed in my home—but there are also times when I want just the right people to come over (the ones I really like). I want to serve the best food, and I want my guests to be impressed—with me and my home. Soon a simple gathering can become all about me. Disappointment can mount when my siblings are a no-show or if the food doesn't turn out the way I want. There is that feeling of emptiness when the event is over and I don't feel I received the accolades I was expecting. This is self-focus—when we do things for people or the church just so we can get our gold star from Jesus. It's what Jesus called self-righteousness, and it can be subtle.

Jesus had an eye for this kind of behavior. He was not afraid to call out the super-religious types who wanted all the attention. In Luke 18, Jesus told a story of two people who went to church. One was a very religious person, a church superstar in Jesus' day, and the other was a tax collector. The tax collector was not exactly a crowd favorite. Tax collectors were considered crooks, criminals, sinners, and oppressors of the people. Anyway, both people found themselves in the Temple. Jesus said,

> "The Pharisee stood by himself and prayed: 'God, I thank you that I am not like other people—robbers, evildoers, adulterers—or even like this tax collector. I fast twice a week and give a tenth of all I get.'
>
> "But the tax collector stood at a distance. He would not even look up to heaven, but beat his breast and said, 'God, have mercy on me, a sinner.'"
>
> (Luke 18:11-13)

Do the Pharisee's words sound familiar? How often have we said something like "Thank God I stand for Jesus and don't drink from a red cup," or "Thank God I'm not like those super-religious people who refuse to drink from red cups." During the season of Advent, Jesus is giving all of us an invitation: discover who you are in me, not in what you do.

AN INVITATION TO RELATIONSHIP

During Advent and Christmas, it's not enough for us to stop overspending or to do a selfish-motive check. Jesus' down-to-earth love is an invitation to a new way of living. Jesus seeks a relationship with us that goes beyond selfish ambition or political banter; it's a relationship of serving, of living out of love. This kind of love is a gift of the Holy Spirit—the ability to love and live as Jesus did. When we embrace a down-to-earth love we are entering into relationship with God—Father, Son, and Holy Spirit. This triune community is not up in heaven bickering and arguing; God's community is in a cosmic dance, a celebration, in which they enjoy one another's presence.

Jesus' down-to-earth love is an invitation to a new way of living. Jesus seeks a relationship with us that goes beyond selfish ambition or political banter; it's a relationship of serving, of living out of love.

Jesus' invitation is a reminder of who we are called to be. It's a seasonal reminder that God is bigger than me, bigger than my whining and my personal problems, bigger than the world's darkness and despair.

If we could truly accept Jesus' invitation—if we were not focused on you or me—what would Advent and Christmas look like? What would it mean to be absolutely, positively, incredibly, down-and-dirty, starting-from-scratch, all about Jesus and the kind of community Jesus calls his followers to be?

What Paul shared with the Philippians and is sharing with us is more than good advice. Paul is describing what we as the body of Christ, we as a faith-filled community, need to be in order to embrace God's love come down. But how do we do that? How do we press in and live out this down-to-earth kind of love?

First we must realize that <u>we do not have to agree to agree</u>. In a world of incessant debate and growing political divides, sometimes the thought of agreement is almost laughable. We are experiencing one of the most contentious political climates in U.S. history. Yet no matter how much it bothers us, we can quickly be sucked into debates, where logic and reasoned rhetoric are exchanged for old-fashioned mudslinging.

When Paul asked these followers of Jesus to agree with one another, he didn't mean they should think or even believe the same things. This was not some kind of call to Christian bipartisanship or even to compromise. Paul simply was asking them to <u>treat one another with love</u>: "Then make my joy complete by being like-minded, having the same love, being one in spirit and of one mind" (Philippians 2:2). When we read the Bible, we discover there often were intense debates among followers of Jesus regarding food sacrificed to idols, circumcision, even whether Gentiles (non-Jews) could really follow Jesus. But even though these early followers argued, the sum total of their identity did not come from what they thought or even what they believed. Their identity as Jesus followers came from how they lived and treated one another.

One of the fathers of our faith, a Carthaginian named Tertullian, when writing about Jesus followers at the end of the second century, described how those early believers treated one another. "But it is mainly the deeds of a love so noble that lead many to put a brand upon us. *See*, they say, *how they love one another*, for they themselves are animated by mutual hatred. See, they say about us, how they are ready even to die for one another."[3] Christians were labeled, branded, because of how well they loved one another. They loved one another so much that they were willing to die for each other. So, what has happened? How has two thousand years so radically changed the way Jesus followers treat one another?

A Covenant of Commitment

One of the differences between the church today and the church of two thousand years ago was the early Christians' commitment to each other. The first Jesus followers treated their commitment to Jesus as a covenant, much like a marriage covenant.

If any earthly relationship is down to earth, it is marriage. Marriage can be, and usually is, a bit messy. When it comes to my own marriage, my husband, Jon, and I do not always agree. When two very opinionated extroverts are joined in the blessed union of marriage, you can expect fireworks—and I am not talking about the good kind. We have come to expect some disagreement. But in our covenant with God and one another, we agree to love each other despite our differing opinions. We agree that we are committed for life, we are in this for the long haul, and we are not going to let our differing opinions diminish the love we have for one another. It is not easy. This level of commitment to unity is hard work. But the work investment is well worth the love we experience in our relationship.

When we make a commitment to follow Jesus, we are saying yes to more than Jesus; we are saying yes to the whole body of Christ. We agree that we are committed for life, we are in this for the long haul, and we are not going to let our differing opinions diminish the love we have for one another. As with marriage, it is not easy. This level of commitment is hard work, but the result is worth it—Jesus' love will be on display in us and through our relationships. Followers of Jesus do not always have to agree to agree, because there is a love we can agree on.

But down-to-earth love is more than agreement. It challenges us to look deep within ourselves at our motivations. Jesus' love does not come from a place of self-preservation or even ambition. Followers of Jesus do not have to win to win. Paul wrote, "Do nothing out of selfish ambition or vain conceit. Rather, in humility value others above yourselves, not looking to your own interests but each of you to the interests of the others" (Philippians 2:3-4). Sometimes as human beings we want to be reassured by God and others that our needs will be met. At the end of the day, many of us have this inner need to know that we are important, that we are right, that we are the best. We want to be the winner.

This need to win is prevalent in American culture, and not just in the multi-billion-dollar sports industry. Even stores market toward our need to win. One recent Advent season, Best Buy was telling us to "win the holidays, shop Best Buy." Although competitiveness is not an evil in and of itself, when competition trumps our relationships, it blinds us to the amazing gift of another. Each person on the planet matters. But when we start to create categories that divide, we lose a sense of the God-created uniqueness of the people around us and the value of the contributions they can make. We classify people as either winners or losers, right or wrong, on this side or that side.

Jesus' contemporaries, even Jesus' own disciples, also struggled with the need to be right and win. The struggle was understandable—after all, they were human. Although Jesus chose twelve people to be his closest companions, he spent intimate time with three. And one day two of them, the brothers James and John, came to Jesus and requested to sit on his right and left side in glory—in other words, "Jesus, when all is said and done, when you become ruler of everything, can we have seats of honor?" It was as if the two brothers were asking for the bronze and silver medals on the Olympic podium. Jesus' reply was not what they wanted to hear.

> "You don't know what you are asking," Jesus said. "Can you drink the cup I drink or be baptized with the baptism I am baptized with?"

> "We can," they answered.

> Jesus said to them, "You will drink the cup I drink and be baptized with the baptism I am baptized with, but to sit at my right or left is not for me to grant. These places belong to those for whom they have been prepared."
>
> (Mark 10:38-40)

Ouch! Although Jesus' response most likely wounded their egos, it may have damaged even more the relationship between the brothers and the rest of the twelve disciples. Scripture reveals the disciples became "indignant"—disgruntled, irritated, angry, offended, mad. Have you ever let your need to win drive a conversation or even a ministry to a point where it wounded someone? I am sure I have. Winning can tear down the fabric of what it means to serve, grow, and live in community—to be the whole and healthy body of Jesus Christ.

Personally, I can make nearly anything a competition. Yet I realize that when I said yes to following Jesus, I also was saying I was okay with being second. I had to be ready to put myself aside, actively placing others above me. I am not suggesting that people should be human doormats. But we do need to be keenly aware of how a competitive spirit can tear apart the body of Christ.

What does it look like to put self aside? How do we accept being second? Perhaps it means confessing that our competition is rooted in pride or selfish ambition. I want to win, and I want to win because I want winning to be about me. Even people of faith want to win, to be right, to be on top, to have all the answers, to have all the power. But the down-to-earth love of Jesus means letting go of pride and power.

What would happen if this Advent we made ourselves second, not only to God but to those around us? For the debates we find ourselves in, maybe it would mean using "yes, and," more often than "no, but." Whatever your personal soapbox, and we all have them, maybe you and I could reach out to a brother or sister in faith who had a different point-of-view—not because we are interested in converting them to our side, but because we want to know who they are and how to best love them. Entering into conversation is not passive, and it is not easy. But it can be a glimpse of heaven coming down to earth.

What would happen if this Advent we made ourselves second, not only to God but to those around us?

One of the many reasons I am honored to serve on staff at Ginghamsburg Church is because of the people. All kinds of people call Ginghamsburg Church their faith home—liberal people, conservative people, LGBTQ, Tea Party members, addicted people, people set free from addiction, folk looking for Jesus, and folk living out Jesus. We have very different beliefs about what it means to call ourselves followers of Jesus Christ.

This week during Advent, my husband, Jon ,and I will open our home to forty people through a ministry we call Open Table. In doing so we have decided to use our home and our table as a space of invitation and reconciliation. Neighbors, friends, church folk, strangers—everyone is invited. At Open Table there will be people known in the community for their conservative rhetoric, along with same-sex married couples, people with means, people without means, people who are degreed and non-degreed. It is a glimpse of God's kingdom. Open Table is there to create unity, love, and a place for healthy conversation. Even though folks at Ginghamsburg have very different ideas about what it means to follow Jesus, we are united in love because we know that Jesus saves, heals, and redeems—not our right beliefs, but the gift of grace that each and every one of us has received through Jesus' death and resurrection.

Paul reminded the Galatians and us,

> So in Christ Jesus you are all children of God through faith, for all of you who were baptized into Christ have clothed yourselves with Christ. There is neither Jew nor Gentile, neither slave nor free, nor is there male and female, for you are all one in Christ Jesus.
>
> (Galatians 3:26-28)

Our unity is found in Jesus. So, is it okay to debate? Yes, absolutely! Faith-filled followers of Jesus Christ can engage in passionate, fierce debate. But debate is not for the sake of "winning" nor for tearing down the competition, but rather for the purpose of building up, understanding, listening, creating unity in the body of Christ.

Avoiding tough subjects can be just as damaging to the body of Christ as mean-spirited debates that create division and hate. We must create spaces of grace in which we can wrestle with the ideas and people that we find most challenge our identity. By creating spaces of grace, we can figure out how to love each other through our differences. Christian theology and practice is not a zero-sum game, with only winners and losers. At the end of the day we may not agree, we may never see eye to eye, but we will stay united because we are on the same team. Followers of Jesus do not have to win to win.

Do Love

Ultimately Paul reminded the followers at Philippi that Jesus' love is an active love. It does not stand by, bottled up and reserved for the right date and time. Jesus' love is actively released through the hands of those who proclaim his name.

> Do nothing out of selfish ambition or vain conceit. Rather, in humility value others above yourselves, not looking to your own interests but each of you to the interests of the others. (Philippians 2:3-4)

What does it look like to place another's interest above our own? Could it mean that we lend a helping hand? Could it mean that we live out Jesus' down-to-earth love?

When surrounded by the spirit of Christmas during "the most wonderful time of the year," generosity and giving a few more dollars to worthwhile charities can seem easy. But I wonder if Paul was talking about something different from our typical concept of charity, involving more than simply writing a check for that end-of-year giving. I believe, in fact, that Paul was directing us to think about the biblical concept of compassion and mercy.

In Luke 10, Jesus told one of his most famous parables to a man who was an expert in religious law. It was the parable of the good Samaritan, a story all about compassion and mercy. A traveler had been mugged, beaten badly, and left for dead at the side of the road. Two people passed him by—a priest and a Levite, both considered in Jesus' day to be highly religious folk—and yet they did nothing to assist the battered man. Jesus said,

> "Then a despised Samaritan came along, and when he saw the man, he felt compassion for him. Going over to him, the Samaritan soothed his wounds with olive oil and wine and bandaged them. Then he put

the man on his own donkey and took him to an inn, where he took care of him. The next day he handed the innkeeper two silver coins, telling him, 'Take care of this man. If his bill runs higher than this, I'll pay you the next time I'm here.'

"Now which of these three would you say was a neighbor to the man who was attacked by bandits?" Jesus asked.

The man replied, "The one who showed him mercy."

Then Jesus said, "Yes, now go and do the same."
(Luke 10:33-37 NLT)

This is what it looks like to lend a helping hand. This is the down-to-earth kind of love that Jesus brought into the world. So, what was Jesus asking of us? He asked us, then and now, to *do love*.

For those of us familiar with the story, this teaching may not seem unsettling. But for Jesus' hearers, it would have been deeply challenging. Jesus was saying to them and to us that our enemy—the foreigner, the outsider, our competition—may actually be the one living out God's love. The Samaritan chose compassion and relationship over rules and religious ritual.

When we think we have Jesus all figured out, when we believe we have chosen the "correct side," Jesus moves on us and declares it's not about choosing a side or winning an argument. It's about love on display, no matter who you are or who is in need.

LOVE IN ACTION

In the twenty-first century, we don't often have an opportunity to pick up a beaten adversary by the side of the road. So, what does it mean for us to be a down-to-earth people? What does it look like for us to be God's love on display?

For those of us at Ginghamsburg, it's a question we always wrestle with, whether we are talking about our work in Sudan or with Syrian refugees, whether we are engaged in ministry with the affluent or with those who lack the physical necessities to live. We continue to explore and discover within our faith community what it really looks like to love Jesus in public, despite our varying political and even theological perspectives. We know that following Jesus is not merely an intellectual exercise. Our brains are part of it, but following Jesus is mostly about actively practicing and living out a down-to-earth love.

Every week I meet people at Ginghamsburg Church who demonstrate this kind of radical love in simple and incredible ways. Doug Powell is a retired schoolteacher who has a lot of energy and a deep desire to live Jesus' love out loud. Doug decided, along with the members of his small group, to start a ministry called "More Than Carpenters." Their mission is simple: lending a helping hand to those in need—single moms, widows, families, anyone whose house needs to be repaired or rehabbed. To ensure that the ministry doesn't just provide a short-term handout, Doug and his team enter into a covenant with those they are helping, that provides opportunity for repair and rehab recipients to learn how to make small repairs on their own in the future. Usually the individuals or families provide the resources; Doug and his team of servants provide the know-how. All of them partner together to take something that was once broken and restore it again. You can imagine that this ministry is about more than fixing leaky faucets. It is about compassion; it is about mercy; it is about discipleship.

This Advent, a group of us will band together and spend hours in the neighborhood sharing the love of Jesus through song. We will gather, eat together, and then go caroling, focusing on the homes of those who need cheer the most—perhaps a person who is living through cancer, or an elderly couple navigating the wife's Alzheimer's, even a neighbor who never seems to come out of the house.

Sometimes we think we have to do something huge to change the world. After all, Ginghamsburg is the church that has raised millions of dollars to fund sustainable humanitarian projects in the Sudan. Yet that is not what we see in Jesus' parable of the good Samaritan. In it, we simply see a man who had compassion, who demonstrated mercy, who was willing to stop along the road to aid someone. Perhaps the first question we should ask ourselves this Advent is simply, "How can I lend a helping hand?"

Lending a helping hand may mean buying extra food at the grocery store for a local food pantry or paying the grocery bill of a stranger. It might mean offering to move some furniture or helping the neighbors down the street clean up their yard. Perhaps it's reaching out to say, "I was wrong. Will you forgive me?" Or, "Hey you look stressed. Is there anything I can do?" Maybe your family or small group can go caroling at the senior center or invite someone over for a home-cooked meal. How can you lend a hand, fix a car, knit a hat, create a piece of beautiful art that will bring someone joy?

This Advent season is an invitation for us to open our hearts to God, to allow God to use our hands in sharing Jesus' love with the people around us. We don't need to have it all figured out. We don't have to agree. We don't have to win. We must simply allow God to use what is in our hands—those basic raw ingredients that God uses to create miracles in our lives and in the lives of others.

Maybe it's true: God can change the world through my mother's homemade pies—Jesus' down-to-earth love on display.

Reflection: Love Does

But a Samaritan, as he traveled, came where the
man was; and when he saw him, he took pity
on him.

(Luke 10:33)

Being part of a church like Ginghamsburg sometimes can lead people to believe doing big things for God is all that matters. Certainly twelve years of investing millions of dollars into Sudan, South Sudan, and Dayton could give one the impression that we followers of Jesus are called to go big or go home at the holidays. But I wonder, in the midst of that big miracle, if we sometimes forget that each miracle begins small—a single act of sacrifice, which is then multiplied by God.

You'd think that Advent and Christmas would be a season when people would be more willing to give and give generously than any other time of the year, but so often the giving that happens around Christmas feels more like charity than it does compassion and mercy. True compassion and mercy are costly, and I'm not talking about writing a check.

In the story we know as the good Samaritan, Jesus reminds us that love knows no boundaries. The Samaritan is despised—a half-breed, a person rejected by the religious faithful—and yet the Samaritan is the hero of the story. For the Samaritan shows mercy and compassion, not only by writing a check (paying for all the medical expenses of the man injured) but also by going out of his way to make sure the man is restored to health. The Samaritan's actions are simple: clean a wound, rent a room, come back to check. And yet these simple actions save the man's life. Too often during Advent and Christmas we forget that small acts of compassion and mercy have as much potential to change lives as Christmas Miracle offerings.

It's the small things that make a difference: the neighbor who clears snow from the elderly couple's driveway, the family that bakes cookies and takes them to the local nursing home (and not just at Christmas), the woman who knits blankets for each new child in the congregation, the man who changes the oil in a single mom's car. These gifts seem small, but when multiplied with God's love they have the power to change lives.

Last year, a friend of mine decided to use Christmas as a great excuse to get to know her neighbors. She is crafty but does not have a lot of extra time. So she made holiday trail mix, placed it in decorative boxes, and wrote a note inviting her neighbors to her church's Christmas Eve worship celebration. She then sent out her husband to deliver the goods. And though none of her neighbors came to worship, every one of them now stops and talks to her and especially to her husband. That one act of love changed the atmosphere in her neighborhood. It was simple, and yet it made an impact on her and on others.

Christmas Miracle offerings are important, but they cannot replace the simple acts of love that Jesus calls us to do. Love more than writes a check; *love does.*

God, thank you for the opportunity to serve you and others through simple acts of love. Remind me on a daily basis how love, through the power of your Holy Spirit, can change the world. Amen.

From *Down to Earth: Devotions for the Season*
by Rachel Billups. Abingdon Press, 2016.

2.
Down to Earth Humility

2.

Down to Earth Humility

Mike

In your relationships with one another, have the same mindset as Christ Jesus:

Who, being in very nature God,
did not consider equality with God something to be
used to his own advantage;
rather, he made himself nothing
by taking the very nature of a servant,
being made in human likeness.
And being found in appearance as a man,
he humbled himself
by becoming obedient to death—
even death on a cross!

(Philippians 2:5-8)

Within weeks of assuming the papacy in March of 2013, Pope Francis dismayed some Catholic traditionalists when he washed two women's feet during a Maundy Thursday mass at a youth prison in Rome. As *The Huffington Post* reported, traditionalists consider the rite a "reenactment of Jesus washing the feet of the twelve apostles before his death," which "thus should be limited only to men." Simply washing the feet of prisoners was startling enough to many Catholic faithful. Traditionally popes have washed the feet of twelve priests, a much "safer" and far more predictable demographic in terms of both behavior and possibly foot cleanliness.[1]

I have been greatly impressed with this pope and inspired to see how Francis, the world leader of the planet's largest Christian denomination, repeatedly puts aside his rights and privilege to demonstrate the mind and humility of Jesus, our down-to-earth God. How can we too live out a down-to-earth humility this Advent?

THE MIND OF JESUS

To experience the new this Advent season, to find our "next," we must let go of the old. Old habits and ways of thinking must be replaced with new. The "mindset" (NIV) and "attitude" (NLT) of Christ Jesus that the Apostle Paul described to the Philippians must supersede our own prejudices, presumptions, and partisan ideologies.

In another one of Paul's letters, he reminded the Christians in Ephesus about the necessity of renewed thinking:

> You were taught, with regard to your former way of life, to put off your old self, which is being corrupted by its deceitful desires; to be made new in the attitude of your minds; and to put on the new self, created to be like God in true righteousness and holiness. (Ephesians 4:22-24)

What is remarkable about this admonition is that it may have been written from a Roman prison cell. Paul knew how to practice what he preached.

The English word *repent* comes from the Greek word *metanoia*, which means a change in mindset or the mind. Our minds control our attitudes, actions, and behaviors. Our thoughts become actions, and our actions become lifestyles. The author of Proverbs reminds us, "As he thinks in his heart, so *is* he" (23:7 NKJV). Our attitudes affect the outcomes of our lives in this world and the world beyond.

Our minds control our attitudes, actions, and behaviors. Our thoughts become actions, and our actions become lifestyles.

One of those key attitudes requires remembering that God is a God of relationships: "In your relationships with one another, have the same mindset as Christ Jesus" (Philippians 2:5). As Rachel mentioned in the previous chapter, Ginghamsburg Church represents a diversity of folks, in both ethnicity and political ideology. In my Facebook newsfeed I frequently find posts from Bruce, a staunchly conservative Tea Party supporter, juxtaposed with those of Matt, a committed political liberal. During one weekend worship celebration, I may be greeted by Beth, a lesbian in her sixties who retired from a male-dominated profession, when she taps me on the shoulder from the row behind me. At the next worship time, I will turn around to find one of our many young married couples, baby carrier parked beside them, seated in the same aisle, representatives of one of the fastest-growing demographics within the church. What binds us together? Our unity in Jesus.

Jesus calls his followers to demonstrate a radically alternative way of living together. In the world, people organize themselves into groups in which people tend to think alike, vote alike, look alike, and share the same economic demographic. But in Christ's kingdom, "There is neither Jew nor Gentile, neither slave nor free, nor is there male and female, for you are all one in Christ Jesus" (Galatians 3:28).

Having the mind of Christ Jesus allows us to see people as Jesus sees them, regardless of political persuasion, sexual orientation, nationality, theological beliefs, or even the lack thereof. Jesus never told his followers, "This is my command; you shall adhere strictly to right doctrinal beliefs and agree with one another on correct political ideology." As a matter of fact, Jesus left us with only one new commandment in all of his teaching.

> "A new command I give you: Love one another. As I have loved you, so you must love one another. By this everyone will know that you are my disciples, if you love one another." (John 13:34-35)

As Jesus' followers, we tend to define people as being "lost" or "saved" doctrinally, but Jesus spoke of God's kingdom relationally. He warned his followers, "Watch out for false prophets. They come to you in sheep's clothing, but inwardly they are ferocious wolves. By their fruit you will recognize them" (Matthew 7:15-16). Jesus saw the truest evidence of faith revealed in our being, not simply in our believing. Please don't misunderstand me. I believe that Jesus is God incarnate in the flesh. But with our profession of faith comes the responsibility to be God's humble servants on earth, not God's judges.

Ultimately it is not our theological positions that determine the authenticity of our faith. True faith is demonstrated through Christlike love. Take a moment to read the thirteen short verses that make up 1 Corinthians 13, which describe that love. Clearly, love supersedes knowledge! In the Epistle to the Ephesians, the Apostle Paul admonishes us,

> Get rid of all bitterness, rage and anger, brawling and slander, along with every form of malice. Be kind and compassionate to one another, forgiving each other, just as in Christ God forgave you. Follow God's example, therefore, as dearly loved children and

walk in the way of love, just as Christ loved us and gave himself up for us as a fragrant offering and sacrifice to God. (Ephesians 4:31–5:2, *emphasis added*)

To have the mind of Christ means a radical reorientation of thinking. A change of mind is a change of heart. A change of heart is a change in behavior. Right thinking precedes right acting. Both require humility.

THE NATURE OF GOD: HUMILITY

Paul reminds us that to know what God is like, we begin by looking at Jesus. Paul wrote to the church at Philippi that Christ Jesus,

being in very nature God, did not consider equality with God something to be used to his own advantage; rather, he made himself nothing by taking the very nature of a servant, being made in human likeness.

(Philippians 2:6-7)

The Greek word for "nature" that Paul used in this text was *morphe*, which means form or shape.[2] Jesus reveals the form or shape of God and what God values, which is the complete antithesis of the cultural gods of power, wealth, war, and privilege held by many of the world's religions throughout the millennia. Christ even reveals the ethos of God as being radically juxtaposed with an Old Testament understanding of a God who commanded his followers to commit genocide against entire communities of people (see 1 Samuel 15:1-3). Jesus, in his Sermon on the Mount, makes critical adjustments to people's perceptions of God.

"You have heard that it was said, 'Eye for eye, and tooth for tooth.' But I tell you, do not resist an evil person. If anyone slaps you on the right cheek, turn to them the other cheek also.... You have heard that it was said, 'Love your neighbor and hate your enemy.'

> But I tell you, love your enemies and pray for those
> who persecute you, that you may be children of your
> Father in heaven. He causes his sun to rise on the evil
> and the good, and sends rain on the righteous and the
> unrighteous." (Matthew 5:38-39, 43-45)

Of course, God doesn't change, but the Incarnation demands that our understanding about God and people must change.

The majority of wars being fought in the world today in the name of religion are based on twisted misunderstandings of God's character. There's little difference between the acts of terror being rationalized in the name of a god who demands *jihad* and Old Testament acts of genocide being justified by Christians. After all, Christians throughout the first two millennia waged our own crusades and burned people at the stake in Jesus' name. Richard Rohr, in his book *The Naked Now*, writes:

> This is why, for so much of our history, we have
> made good bedfellows with kings, queens, dictators
> and repressive regimes. We perceive that God is
> a god who fights on our side, favors us over other
> people, preserves our way of living and supports our
> nationalistic interest.[3]

Jesus was not the Messiah people expected. They were looking for a candidate—someone who today we might call a political pundit—to "make Israel great again." We hear the same echoes reverberating throughout our own landscape. Jesus' own disciples, enmeshed in the upheaval caused by Roman occupation and the burden of taxation, could be caught up in the political frenzy. Even after the disciples had experienced the Resurrection firsthand, they asked Jesus, "Lord, are you at this time going to restore the kingdom to Israel?" (Acts 1:6). Judas's betrayal of Jesus was about much more than the thirty pieces of silver he received for that treasonous act; in fact, because of Jesus' failure to take political action against Rome, Judas refused to believe that Jesus was God's messiah. The mother of two disciples came to Jesus and asked if her sons could have the benefit of political office when Jesus assumed power (Matthew 20:20). We would do well to take notice of Jesus' response on that occasion: "You don't know what you are asking," followed by the ultimate question of discipleship, "Can you drink the cup I am going to drink?" (v. 22).

Christians sometimes assume that Jesus had superhuman powers to do the miraculous things that he pulled off. But Paul reminds us that Jesus emptied himself of the powers of divinity, "taking the very nature of a servant" by becoming completely human (Philippians 2:7). The theological term for his emptying himself of divine powers but not of his divinity is *kenosis*. In this sense Jesus had no advantage over you and me; he did it because of his total dependence upon God. We can see this dependence when Jewish leaders began to persecute Jesus right after he healed the invalid at the spa pools of Bethesda. When the leaders questioned Jesus about his willful breaking of the Jewish law by healing on the Sabbath, he responded,

> "Very truly I tell you, the Son can do nothing by him-
> self; he can do only what he sees his Father doing,
> because whatever the Father does the Son also does."
>
> (John 5:19)

Jesus emptied himself of all the powers and privileges of divinity. He entered into the brokenness of humanity that we in our sinfulness create and into painful situations that we don't create. Jesus revealed a God of downward mobility, to the point that he was born into a working-class family in an obscure, remote village. Some archaeologists note that Nazareth is not mentioned in ancient Jewish sources earlier than the third century A.D. At the time of Jesus it might have had a maximum population of fewer than five hundred.[4] The village was likely made up of peasant laborers who served as day workers in the prosperous Roman city of Sepphoris, located approximately three miles from Nazareth. Joseph and Jesus might have found work in Sepphoris during an ambitious first-century building program initiated by Herod Antipas.[5]

❭ Jesus was born into an ethnic minority that had experienced the ravages of persecution and genocide through the millennia of their existence. He experienced firsthand what it meant to live as a refugee in Africa for two years, as his family fled persecution by Herod. Jesus revealed a God who identifies with the internally displaced refuges in Darfur, and the families escaping the horrors being carried out in modern-day Syria. God stands with the more than 68,000 unaccompanied children who are being held at the U.S. southern border, who have come fleeing the violence in Honduras, El Salvador, and Guatemala.[6] God, as revealed in Jesus, comes into the races and faces of oppressed people.

The prophet Isaiah spoke of the Suffering Servant who would come:

> He was oppressed and afflicted, / yet he did not open his mouth;.../ By oppression and judgment he was taken away. / Yet who of his generation protested? / For he was cut off from the land of the living; / for the transgression of my people he was punished. / He was assigned a grave with the wicked, / and with the rich in his death, / though he had done no violence, / nor was any deceit in his mouth. (Isaiah 53:7-9)

Jesus himself claimed to be that servant when he read his mission statement from Isaiah 61 in his hometown synagogue:

> The Spirit of the Sovereign LORD is on me, / because the LORD has anointed me / to proclaim good news to the poor. / He has sent me to bind up the brokenhearted, / to proclaim freedom for the captives / and release from darkness for the prisoners, / to proclaim the

year of the LORD's favor / and the day of vengeance of
our God, / to comfort all who mourn, / and provide
for those who grieve in Zion— / to bestow on them
a crown of beauty / instead of ashes, / the oil of joy
/ instead of mourning, / and a garment of praise
instead / of a spirit of despair. (Isaiah 61:1-3)

We must confess that those of us who profess Jesus as Messiah are
often guilty of reducing his mission to a self-serving, otherworldly,
personalized faith. We neglect the weightier call to work against
injustice and alleviate suffering in the world. Jesus reveals a down-to-
earth God who is committed to a down-to-earth mission!

THE GREAT SIN: PRIDE

Before we can clothe ourselves in the down-to-earth humility that
Jesus modeled, we must first deal with arguably the greatest of our sins,
pride. C. S. Lewis, in his classic book *Mere Christianity*, hit the nail on
the head when he wrote:

> The vice I am talking of is Pride or Self-Conceit: and
> the virtue opposite to it, in Christian morals, is called
> Humility.... According to Christian teachers, the
> essential vice, the utmost evil, is Pride. Unchastity,
> anger, greed, drunkenness, and all that, are mere
> fleabites in comparison: it was through Pride that the
> devil became the devil: Pride leads to every other vice:
> it is the complete anti-God state of mind."[7]

The Old Testament story of Uzziah is one of Scripture's cautionary
tales about what can happen when hubris replaces humility. Uzziah was
sixteen years old when he became king of Judah. We are told that "he
did what was right in the eyes of the LORD, just as his father Amaziah
had done" (2 Chronicles 26:4). Uzziah set his heart to seek God and

was wise enough to put himself under the spiritual mentorship of Zechariah. We read of Uzziah, "As long as he sought the LORD, God gave him success" (v. 5). As a result, Uzziah grew in wealth and political influence.

But wealth and success should come with a warning label. The increase in wealth brings an inherent danger of "heart pride" and forgetting the source of our blessings. Moses, after leading the Israelites out of Egypt and through the wilderness, had warned the people of this. When they came into the land of promise, manna would no longer be the daily staple. They would build fine houses and gain wealth. "But remember the LORD your God," said Moses, "for it is he who gives you the ability to produce wealth" (Deuteronomy 8:18).

> Wealth and success should come with a warning label. The increase in wealth brings an inherent danger of "heart pride" and forgetting the source of our blessings.

Uzziah did not remember. Success caused him to turn to the Dark Side. "His fame spread far and wide, for he was greatly helped until he became powerful. But after Uzziah became powerful, his pride led to his downfall. He was unfaithful to the LORD his God" (2 Chronicles 26:15-16).

As Jesus followers, we must repent of prideful hubris that elevates our own sense of righteousness over others. Jesus cuts right to the heart of our hypocrisy. When questioned by the Pharisees and scribes about his disciples not following "the traditions of the elders," Jesus declared,

"Isaiah was right when he prophesied about you hypocrites; as it is written: / 'These people honor me with their lips, / but their hearts are far from me. / They worship me in vain; / their teachings are merely human rules.' / You have let go of the commands of God and are holding on to human traditions." (Mark 7:6-8)

Sadly, U.S. presidential campaigns provide examples every four years of how easily Christians can prioritize political hubris over Christlike humility and love. Last Lent, with the elections in mind, I issued a challenge: instead of giving up social media or red wine or chocolate for Lent, why not give up being a jerk? Think of the difference you and I could make in our communities by refusing to indulge in mudslinging and political carping. Imagine what would happen if, instead, we acted on Jesus' directive to "love your enemies, do good to those who hate you, bless those who curse you, pray for those who mistreat you" (Luke 6:27-28).

Yes, we must admit, we who sin are guilty of casting stones. Our self-righteous indignation and critical judgment of others do not honor God or build faith in the lives of others.

The great Indian leader Mahatma Gandhi remained a devoted Hindu throughout his life, even though he seriously considered the way of Jesus. However, his experience with Christian missionaries in India and their general alliance with the politics of colonialism made him doubtful that Christianity had any unique claim to the truth. Gandhi could see the grave contradiction between the way Christians lived and spoke and the "law of love" he found in what he called the "true message of Jesus" found in the Sermon on the Mount.

The Christian writer Thomas Merton wrote, "Our job is to love others without stopping to inquire whether or not they are worthy."[8] Giving up being a jerk may be harder than giving up chocolate, but think of the difference it could make in our lives and the lives of others.

Humility allows us as Jesus followers to elevate our love for God and people over allegiance to institutional religious, nationalistic, and political traditions. Until we do, is it any wonder that so much of our contemporary Christian witness is falling on deaf ears? We will have an impact when we show the world what it means to value people over partisanship.

AN UPSIDE-DOWN KINGDOM

Nineteenth-century English author Lewis Carroll wrote *Through the Looking-Glass* as the sequel to *Alice's Adventures in Wonderland*. In that sequel, Alice steps into a mirror in her living room and finds that everything is backward. That's similar to the upside-down way Jesus portrayed the kingdom of God, which is so unlike the kingdoms of the world.

As King of kings and Lord of lords, who but Jesus had more right to use power and prestige for personal gain? Yet Jesus entered the world into an oppressed class of humanity, assuming the lowest position in the Roman world. Despite Jesus' supreme divinity, the Apostle Paul writes that "he made himself nothing by taking the very nature of a servant, being made in human likeness" (Philippians 2:7). For "servant," Paul uses the Greek word *doulos*, which literally means "slave." In his final kind act toward his disciples on planet earth, the Master of the universe humbled himself to take on the role of a *doulos*, willingly washing the disciples' filthy feet.

Jesus' Sermon on the Mount (Matthew 5–7) begins with the Beatitudes and then expands on them. Taken alongside his remarkable teaching about Judgment Day in Matthew 25, these words further reveal the upside-down, countercultural nature of God's kingdom.

- To be blessed, you must bless others.
- To be forgiven, you must forgive others.

- To avoid being judged, you must not judge others.
- The first will be last, and the last will be first.
- You must lose yourself to find yourself.
- You must first give before you can receive.
- The poor will inherit the kingdom of heaven.
- The meek will inherit the earth.
- Peacemakers will be called children of God.
- The hungry are fed.
- Safe water is provided for the thirsty.
- The sick are ministered to.
- The prisoners are visited.
- The refugee is given shelter.
- The poor are clothed.
- There is neither Jew nor Gentile, neither slave nor free, neither male nor female, for all are one in Christ.

In the spring of 2009, I was privileged to travel with Ambassador Tony Hall as part of a peace delegation. It was my third trip to the Holy Land, and I was shocked to find on this occasion that a wall had been built around the town of Bethlehem, preventing free travel for the Palestinians living inside the walls. The wall's purpose was apparently to segregate and isolate the area's ethnic-religious populations, which included more than 170,000 Palestinians. It's hard to imagine the economic and humanitarian toll that the wall has made on those residents. Palestinian homes have been bulldozed and farmland confiscated by the Jewish government. I understand that Israel has the right to exist and defend itself from the real threats of radical Arab extremists, but Palestinians have an equal right.

It's doubtful whether Jesus' birth could have taken place in today's Bethlehem, because Mary and Joseph would have been denied entrance. You might think I have just taken an unwelcome political turn at this juncture of my Advent accounting, but we dare not "spiritualize"

Jesus' down-to-earth mission. Jesus had a very upside-down, earthy purpose in the hypercharged political climate of first-century Palestine that holds equally true for today, as Paul explained in his Letter to the Ephesians:

> For he himself [Jesus] is our peace, who has made the two groups one and has destroyed the barrier, *the dividing wall of hostility*, by setting aside in his flesh the law with its commands and regulations. His purpose was to create in himself one new humanity out of the two, thus making peace, and in one body to reconcile both of them to God through the cross, by which he put to death their hostility. He came and preached peace to you who were far away and peace to those who were near. For through him we both have access to the Father by one Spirit. (Ephesians 2:14-18, *emphasis added*)

The Kingdom movement of Jesus tears down all walls of division. Jesus followers are called to build bridges over the global ideological chasms that divide us!

Jesus followers are called to build bridges over the global ideological chasms that divide us!

A recent article in *The New York Times* used similar language. Titled "Pope Francis' Popularity Bridges Great Divides," the article stated that Pope Francis's influence has spread further than his global Catholic audience. The pope's fans include people from all backgrounds including Muslims, Hindus, evangelicals, and even atheists. "I believe he's a world leader," said Sasha Datta, a practicing Hindu who was hoping to see Francis in Washington on the pope's summer American tour. "His openness, his ability to not shy away from real issues—I see a lot of hope when I see people like Pope Francis."[9]

As we have seen, for many people Pope Francis is the antithesis of what they expect to see in a global leader of influence. He refuses to live in an ornate, extravagant palace and instead chooses a room in a more practical Vatican guesthouse. Francis is seen frequently eating with the poor or washing the feet of prisoners. He calls for grace for the divorced and has stated when asked about homosexuality, "Who am I to judge?" Even the atheist Bill Maher has made positive statements about this pope and the stands he has taken for the poor and on climate change. Regarding climate change, Maher said, "I think it's just awesome that this pope took on this issue. I love that Boehner invited him to talk to Congress."[10] Whatever our views on specific issues, the point is that Pope Francis represents an upside-down, kingdom of God worldview. Oh, that the world might see Jesus, born anew this Christmas, in the lives of his followers.

REACHING THE WORLD FOR CHRIST

The world will begin to believe in Jesus as it sees those who call themselves Christians acting like Jesus. It is essential that our lives and our churches demonstrate these essential upside-down, kingdom of God attributes if we want to reach the world for Christ.

At Ginghamsburg Church, for example, our commitment to change the world one life at a time really began to take off by the mid-1980s. As a result, we needed to add a second, then a third, and then a fourth worship service. We purchased property from the surrounding farms to make room for additional parking. Our little country community comprised only twenty-two houses, but there was a traffic jam every Sunday morning that required the assistance of two county sheriff deputies. I remember calling my grandfather, who had been the primary influence in my commitment to Jesus, and sharing with him the great success we were experiencing in the ministry. I have never forgotten his words: "Pride goes before destruction, / a haughty spirit before a fall" (Proverbs 16:18).

Indeed, pride may be the biggest barrier to reaching the world for Christ. When the first human beings described in the Bible acted outside the will of God, they were inspired by the serpent's words: "You will not certainly die... For God knows that when you eat from [the fruit tree] your eyes will be opened, *and you will be like God*, knowing good and evil" (Genesis 3:4-5, *emphasis added*). We act as if we know better than God when we fail to do as God commanded: "Administer true justice; show mercy and compassion to one another. Do not oppress the widow or the fatherless, the foreigner or the poor" (Zechariah 7:9-10). We act as our own god when we judge others and when we fail to release the resources that God has entrusted to our hands so that others may find life.

Jesus showed laser-focus when he laid out the parameters for Judgment Day:

> "For I was hungry and you gave me something to eat, I was thirsty and you gave me something to drink, I was a stranger and you invited me in, I needed clothes and you clothed me, I was sick and you looked after me, I was in prison and you came to visit me.... Truly I tell you, whatever you did for one of the least of these brothers and sisters of mine, you did for me."
>
> (Matthew 25:35-36, 40)

And likewise whatever we failed to do, we failed to do for Jesus. Either way, when we rationalize any directive of Jesus we are intentionally saying, "I know better than God!"

One of the best times to reach the world for Christ is during Advent and Christmas. Since 2004, Ginghamsburg Church has been committed to a mission emphasis called *Christmas Is Not Your*

Birthday.[11] The idea behind our program is for each family to spend only half as much on themselves for Christmas and then give an equal amount (the other half) to a cause that honors Jesus' birth. Did you catch the phrase "equal amount"? Christians are often guilty of getting caught up in the marketing frenzy that feeds our materialistic impulses and increases the burden of debt, and believe me, I am by no means immune to this seasonal affluenza.

Since that initial commitment in 2004, our people have given nearly eight million dollars through what we call the Christmas Miracle Offering. Our focus has been on creating sustainable agriculture programs, bringing safe water sources, providing children's education through building schools, and eliminating malaria in Darfur and South Sudan. In Darfur, the offering has fed more than 15,970 households, returning families to the farming business. Also 290 schools have been built or rehabilitated, cumulatively serving nearly 35,000 students. Nineteen safe-water yards have been implemented to provide water for tens of thousands as well as for their livestock. In South Sudan, more schools and safe-water initiatives are reaching vulnerable communities, and the distribution of 30,000 treated mosquito nets, accompanied by education on their effective usage, is saving lives from the killer but preventable disease of malaria.

The water contamination crisis that started in Flint, Michigan, in April 2014 has brought water concerns closer to home for Americans. But did you know that, globally, unclean water kills a child every twenty seconds? It is the cause for more deaths than AIDS, malaria, and tuberculosis combined. One in every six people worldwide has no access to safe water.[12] In some areas of Darfur where we have been working, women and children spend as many as eight hours a day walking to and from water sources to get clean water. This is why many of the water projects that I mentioned have been implemented near schools, eliminating the need for vulnerable children to travel or miss out on the opportunity for an education.

I am thankful for the thousands of churches, schools, and clubs that have taken on a similar Christmas challenge, making significant differences in their communities and throughout the world. Even my own alma mater, North College Hill High School in Cincinnati, has raised almost $50,000 for our work in Sudan. This is especially remarkable given that 100 percent of the students in that school receive free breakfasts, and 90 percent participate in the free-lunch program.

Jon Morgan is the pastor of our Fort McKinley Campus, in Dayton, Ohio, in an at-risk community often known for its drug houses, crime, and poverty. Ginghamsburg merged in 2008 with what was then Fort McKinley United Methodist Church, a dying congregation of about forty aging people who commuted from various communities. The church now hosts a vibrant and diverse worshiping community of more than four hundred attendees weekly who reach their community in amazing and incarnational ways. Pastor Jon gives our people a great reminder of what it means to be down-to-earth humble servants: "Don't take advantage of your position, but position your advantage." In other words, use the platform God has given you to speak out and act on behalf of others. Speak out and act for those who lack privilege!

Advent is the celebration of God's true light that has broken into the world's darkness in the birth of Jesus, reminding us that we are part of a kingdom of God movement that is tearing down the walls that stand between us. God is doing a new thing. Jesus said, "Blessed are the meek, for they will inherit the earth." In the Spirit of humility, allow the living Jesus to come into your life anew this Christmas. Dare to love others as God loves you!

Reflection:
A Picture of Humility

Humble yourselves before the Lord, and he will lift you up.

(*James 4:10*)

Four times a year I travel to Cincinnati, Ohio, to the Transfiguration Spirituality Center (TSC). The TSC not only houses individuals and groups on retreat, but also is home to an Episcopal religious order for women. Each time I go there on retreat, I eat meals with the sisters, and some of the meals are in silence. For an extrovert who loves meeting new people, I found this practice annoying at first. However, I soon learned that something happens in the silence. Not only do I find myself listening more intently, but my eyes are opened to what is happening around me.

These sisters care for one another carefully and intentionally. The eldest in the group is the feeblest, and although she is able to get her own plate of food, multiple sisters help her be seated and tend to her needs. Watching her, I see the humility baked into her daily choices—

a common wardrobe worn for years, no signs of makeup or nail polish, a habit that covers her whitening hair. When I see her, I think to myself, "Could I ever be so humble as to lose my identity to Jesus?"

I walk in wearing heels, makeup, sometimes even ripped jeans. Seeing the simple garb of the sisters, my inner rebel screams out, "No way!" After all, my outward appearance expresses my identity, and these sisters are distinguishable only by the sizes and shapes of their faces and bodies. It seems like a grave sacrifice, losing their uniqueness to gain a closer connection with God and one another.

The humility in those decisions nearly takes my breath away. I ask myself, "How? Why?" As I continue to watch the sisters, I realize that when I'm near them, I feel joy and the presence of the holy. I don't believe it's because they are inherently holy; rather, their humility gives the Holy Spirit space to shine in and through them.

I don't believe Jesus is asking me to give up my favorite pair of jeans or shoes, but I do believe he asks me to hand over my identity for a new identity, an identity in which I and anyone else willing to follow Jesus are shaped and formed into their best selves, their best Spirit-filled selves. Inherent in the handoff is humility. The sisters are an invitation to a simpler life. Each time I visit, their humility calls me and challenges me to wrestle with my assumptions about what it means to follow Jesus.

In today's Scripture, James reminds us that humility is a prerequisite for being "lifted up." Glory is never the goal, but if we are lifted without humility, then the only thing people see is us. Humility reveals a deeper truth and identity. Humility is an invitation to a new way of living. I do not believe I will ever be called to live in a convent with a group of sisters, but I know they help shape my vision of what humility looks like.

What pictures of humility do you see? How can you spend time with people who challenge your vision of humility? What keeps you from handing your identity over to Jesus?

Lord Jesus, you are our ultimate picture of humility. Our pride so often keeps us from deepening our relationship with you and others. Help us to release our identity to you, so that we can fully experience our truest God-centered selves, in Jesus' name. Amen.

From *Down to Earth: Devotions for the Season*
by Rachel Billups. Abingdon Press, 2016.

3.

Down to Earth Lifestyle

3.

Down to Earth Lifestyle

Mike

When Joseph woke up, he did what the angel of the Lord had
commanded him and took Mary home as his wife.

(Matthew 1:24)

God speaks to people through dreams, even though most of us
would prefer an audible voice booming from heaven. An audible voice
would give full assurance that the directive was from God and was not
the nocturnal consequence of the previous evening's spicy cuisine.

It was in a dream that an angel appeared to Joseph. We can read
the story in Matthew 1:18-25. In Jesus' time, marriage took place at a
relatively young age. Men often waited until they were eighteen, an age
when they would have been established in a trade that would enable
them to support a new family. Women married as soon as they were
physically able, around the age of twelve or thirteen. Marriages were
usually arranged by the parents. There was a period following the

arrangement called "betrothal," and, following that, the wedding ceremony was held. It was after the ceremony, and presumably not before, that the marriage union was consummated.

But before the ceremony Joseph learned that his betrothed, Mary, was pregnant. You can imagine the absolute shock and sense of betrayal that Joseph must have felt. Matthew makes it clear that Joseph had been faithful in practicing physical restraint and that because he "did not want to expose her to public disgrace, he had in mind to divorce her quietly" (Matthew 1:19). Public exposure could have resulted in execution by stoning, which is still carried out in some countries in the Middle East today. This practice was based in a literal rendering of Scripture:

> If, however, the charge is true and no proof of the young woman's virginity can be found, she shall be brought to the door of her father's house and there the men of her town shall stone her to death. She has done an outrageous thing in Israel by being promiscuous in her father's house. You must purge the evil from among you. (Deuteronomy 22:20-21)*

Take a moment to put yourself in Joseph's shoes. He was obviously devastated, definitely angry, but he chose to live above cultural-religious bigotry to seek the best way out of a broken trust. Even a man in love, with great faith, knows that it takes two to make a baby. And Joseph was not one of the two.

---

*This horrendous act was carried out and continues to be carried out even in the case of rape! Sharmeen Obaid-Chinoy was awarded an Oscar at the 2016 ceremonies for the documentary short entitled, *A Girl in the River*. This film is an excellent documentary exposing the practice of honor killings in orthodox Muslim communities in Pakistan. *USA Today* reported that in 2015, approximately five hundred people, mostly women and girls, were murdered in honor killings for "alleged infidelity and refusing to submit to arranged marriages." Women's rights groups estimate the numbers to be far higher. Read more: "Oscar-winning film casts light on honor killings in Pakistan," by Naila Inayat, *USA Today*, March 1, 2016, http://www.usatoday.com/story/news /world/2016/02/27/oscar-nominated-film-casts-light-honor-killings-pakistan/81012892/).

That was when Joseph had the dream. In it, an angel appeared and told him to take Mary as his wife. Now, I don't know about you, but I would want something more than a dream to inform me that "the Holy Spirit did it!" But a dream was all that Joseph was given, and by faith Joseph acted on that dream: "When Joseph woke up, he did what the angel of the Lord commanded him and took Mary home as his wife" (Matthew 1:24).

You and I can so easily "spiritualize" the events surrounding the Christmas story, but there was nothing about the Holy Family that would remove them from the down-to-earth realities of everyday life. This was true for Joseph, and it's true for all of us in following the costly lifestyle of discipleship. Jesus said, "Whoever wants to be my disciple must deny themselves and take up their cross daily and follow me. For whoever wants to save their life will lose it, but whoever loses their life for me will save it" (Luke 9:23-24). Dietrich Bonhoeffer, the German theologian who was martyred by hanging in the dreaded Flossenburg concentration camp, put it this way: "When Christ calls a man, he bids him come and die."[1]

ACTIVATING GOD-SIZED DREAMS

As we read in the Book of Acts, the ability to dream God-sized dreams demonstrates the reality of the Holy Spirit's presence with us and in us: "In the last days, God says, / I will pour out my Spirit on all people. / Your sons and daughters will prophesy, / your young men will see visions, / your old men will dream dreams" (Acts 2:17). When God gives a vision, God will make provision! God's Spirit resources us to live faith-based lifestyles and carry out kingdom of God missions. This is what Jesus meant when he said, "Very truly I tell you, whoever believes in me will do the works I have been doing, and they will do even greater things than these, because I am going to the Father" (John 14:12). Jesus followed this with the promise of the Father sending the Holy Spirit to be an "advocate" to help us and be with us forever (v. 16).

Joseph's obedience to the angel's directive through his dream shows the critical nature of faith and faith's application in daily life. Jesus reminded a man about the necessity of faith when the man asked if Jesus had the capability to heal his son, saying,

"If you can do anything, take pity on us and help us."
"'If you can'?" said Jesus. "Everything is possible for one who believes."

The man's response has become a lifelong personal prayer for me.

"I do believe; help me overcome my unbelief!"
(Mark 9:22b-24).

In Matthew's accounting of this event, Jesus told his disciples they were powerless to meet the needs of this man's young son because of their near absence of faith. He went on to say, "Truly I tell you, if you have faith as small as a mustard seed, you can say to this mountain, 'Move from here to there,' and it will move. Nothing will be impossible for you" (Matthew 17:20-21).

Faith is perhaps the most underutilized asset in the church. Last Christmas, Pastor Rachel Billups gave my wife, Carolyn, and me a gift card to one of our favorite local restaurants. We both expressed our gratitude, but then Carolyn reminded me that we still hadn't used the gift card to the same restaurant that Rachel had given us the year before. How many of you are guilty of the same omission? Apparently you and I are not the only ones. In the United States alone, forty-four billion dollars of unredeemed gift cards have been accumulating since 2008.[2] As with our Christian faith, we have too often failed to redeem what has already been paid for with a price!

It is just too easy to hold to a form of faith, and yet at the same time to deny faith's power. Jesus encountered a man at the healing pools of Bethesda who had lain in the same state of paralysis for thirty-eight years. (Take a moment to read the account in the fifth chapter of the Gospel of John.) Honing in with laserlike precision, Jesus posed a question that penetrated to the root of the man's condition: "Do you want to get well?" (John 5:6).

Jesus knows the nature of our hearts. Rationalization, pride, deception, and procrastination—he sees them all. As Jeremiah put it, "The heart is deceitful above all things and beyond cure. / Who can understand it?" (Jeremiah 17:9). Like the man at Bethesda, we learn to become comfortable in our current status, no matter how miserable, and resist a down-to-earth, kingdom-of-God lifestyle. Our tepid forms of institutional Christianity deny the gospel's power to bring good news to the poor and freedom for the oppressed. We so easily gloss over the passages that call us to sell our possessions and give to the poor. We surround ourselves in comfortable cocoons of easy and safe systems of belief instead of following the living Christ into the trenches to attack the world's pain.

Jesus knows the nature of our hearts. Rationalization, pride, deception, and procrastination—he sees them all.

We hope for miracles, but remember that every miracle has two components: divine intervention and human responsibility. For a real miracle to take place, we must act on God's directive, as Joseph did when he followed the angel's command and took Mary as his wife.

Faith always requires a corresponding action. When Jesus' disciples asked where the food would come from to feed over five thousand families, his response was, "You give them something to eat" (Matthew 14:16). When ten lepers came asking Jesus for healing, "he said, 'Go, show yourselves to the priests.' And as they went, they were cleansed" (Luke 17:14). Like Joseph with his dream, like the disciples feeding the five thousand, when the lepers acted on their faith, a miracle happened.

Making faith commitments on a daily basis has a cumulative effect that will give exponential results—maybe even miracles—for the rest of your life and beyond.

A DOWN-TO-EARTH VISION

The Syrian refugee crisis that began in 2011 came to the forefront of the world's attention by the summer of 2015. That June, the United Nations reported that nearly sixty million people worldwide had been forcibly displaced—one in every 122 human beings on Planet Earth was now either a refugee, internally displaced, or seeking asylum.[3]

Although 2015 press coverage focused our attention on Syrian refugees in the Middle East and entering Europe, the crisis was and remains a global phenomenon. As the U.N. report noted, the number of people fleeing had exploded because, since 2011, fifteen conflicts around the globe had erupted or reignited, including eight in Africa, three in the Middle East, three in Asia, and one in Europe. The Americas were also affected, with Central Americans fleeing to the U.S. to escape gang violence or other forms of persecution.[4] The news reports were troubling to me; the immensity of the crisis felt overwhelming.

I am passionate about the daily practice of contemplative listening to the inner voice of the Spirit. If the weather is nice, I usually sit on our deck in the evening with a glass of wine, looking out over the fishpond in our backyard. Squirrels, robins, and chickadees gather, with the resident chipmunk making a quorum. The sights and sounds help carry my imagination beyond our suburban neighborhood. One late September evening, while I was enjoying the colors of the changing seasons, the image of a widely circulated photo appeared suddenly and inexplicably in my mind. It was a picture of a drowned Syrian toddler, following his family's failed attempt to escape from Syria to Greece by boat, who was sprawled face-down on a Turkish beach. Feeling a deep sense of urgency, I knew this was more than an idle thought and sensed a nudging from God.

I thought of how the people at Ginghamsburg Church and beyond had responded to the mission emphasis called *Christmas Is Not Your Birthday*, which encouraged Jesus followers to make Christmas a season of sacrificial giving to the needs of others. Now it was as if the Spirit was speaking to me and saying, "What if people from across the country rallied to meet the needs of refugees fleeing violence, ethnic cleansing, and religious genocide?"

It was 7:20 p.m. and the workday was over, but I decided to call my friend Thomas Kemper, the General Secretary of the United Methodist General Board of Global Ministries, based in New York City. The United Methodist Committee on Relief (UMCOR) within Global Ministries has been Ginghamsburg's ten-year partner for our nearly eight-million-dollar investment in providing sustainable agriculture, safe water, schools, and treated malaria nets for people in Darfur, Sudan, and South Sudan. When I called Thomas, I assumed I would reach his voice mail and was surprised when he answered.

I quickly sketched out an idea taking shape in my mind—that *Christmas Is Not Your Birthday* could be adapted to empower hundreds of churches globally to resource efforts to serve refugees and the communities that host them. Twelve days later, I found myself on an airplane with colleague Karen Smith heading to New York to meet with Thomas, his team, and leaders from The United Methodist Publishing House on a preliminary plan and resources that could start bringing that God-prompting into reality. Shortly after the New York meeting, United Methodist Communications in Nashville also joined the initiative. Two weeks later, Ginghamsburg's chief storyteller Dan Bracken flew to Beirut, Lebanon, to create a documentary with a Lebanese film crew concerning the plight of Syrian refugees. Following the filming, a double-suicide bombing killed forty-three and wounded more than two hundred in the working-class neighborhood of Bourj el-Barajneh where the crew had worked, further fueling Dan's desire to create a story that would compel Jesus followers to act.

United Methodist Global Ministries stepped up through a mission program called The Advance to provide a centralized collection point for financial gifts given toward the crisis. This past Christmas, churches and individuals gave nearly one million dollars to Advance #3022144, as well as to other Global Ministries initiatives serving refugees and migrants.

Christians have not always been so generous toward the plight of immigrants, and yet the Bible contains many stories about people of foreign lands. In Acts we read that on the Day of Pentecost, a number of different nations were represented. The Old Testament is filled with declarations as to how God's people were to treat the foreigners among them. Exodus 22:21 mandates, "Do not mistreat or oppress a foreigner, for you were foreigners in Egypt." Exodus 23:9 and Leviticus 19:33-34 sing the same refrain.

We humbly remember that, as a young child, Jesus himself was a refugee in Egypt when his parents desperately tried to save him from genocide. Christmas is not our birthday; it's Jesus' birthday. How best can we give sacrificially for the one who sacrificed his all for us?

The Christmas season reminds us that Christians are to form a community of light in the midst of darkness—a broad, thriving, and investing community through which God pours heaven's resources and purposes into Planet Earth.

Do you feel the Spirit nudging you to make a difference in the heartbreaking worldwide refugee crisis? I encourage you to view Dan Bracken's story at ginghamsburg.org/miracleoffering and to visit umcor.org (Global Refugee/Migration Response) for contribution information.

Even after forty-plus years of ministry, God is still working on me. But one lesson I have learned is that when the Spirit calls, don't wait until tomorrow; otherwise our hearts will grow cold, and the forgetting will start. I have also learned that no matter how crazy a prompting may sound, if the call is from the Spirit, God will provide all the help and resources needed to bring it to reality.

THE GOD OF THE TOWEL

The night before his arrest and execution, Jesus demonstrated what it means to live a servant lifestyle. The dusty Palestinian roads combined with sandals being the footwear of necessity made footwashing an essential tradition before community meals. It was a job usually done by a house servant or slave, but that evening Jesus got up from the table and began to wash the feet of his disciples. Reading the story in John 13:1-17, we can see how shocked the disciples were. In that act, Jesus was teaching them that the Lord of the universe did not come to be served but to serve others in the humblest of tasks.

Jesus taught similar lessons many times, but the disciples, like all of us, were quick to forget. One day when they were jostling for position in the Kingdom, Jesus reminded them,

> "You know that the rulers of the Gentiles lord it over them, and their high officials exercise authority over them. Not so with you. Instead, whoever wants to become great among you must be your servant, and whoever wants to be first must be your slave—just as the Son of Man did not come to be served, but to serve and give his life as ransom for many"
> (Matthew 20:25-28).

Jesus' down-to-earth demonstration of a servant lifestyle was a radical contrast to the disciples arguing among themselves about greatness. The idea of washing one another's feet would have never crossed their minds. Look at Jesus' comments after he finished the demonstration, and be sure to notice the order of wording and how he changed it to make a point.

> "Do you understand what I have done for you? . . . You call me 'Teacher' and 'Lord,' and rightly so, for that is what I am. Now that I, your Lord and Teacher, have washed your feet, you also should wash one another's feet." (John 13:12-14)

Note that Jesus' disciples referred to him as being first their teacher and then their Lord, but Jesus described himself as being first and foremost their Lord, the absolute and ultimate authority. In making the point, Jesus was telling his disciples that faith can never be separated from a down-to-earth lifestyle of compassionate action. A commitment to follow Jesus commits one to a lifestyle of service. Jesus put it this way:

> "Very truly I tell you, no servant is not greater than his master, nor is a messenger greater than the one who sent him. Now that you know these things, you will be blessed if you do them." (vv. 16-17).

Dorothy Stang, who was from my hometown of Dayton, Ohio, committed her life early to serve God as part of a worldwide organization known as the Sisters of Notre Dame de Namur. She spent some time teaching in the United States, then served the poorest of the poor in Brazil's Amazon Basin, where she was outspoken on behalf of the environment. Dorothy's work with the poor farmers in Brazil made her a threat to the lumber barons who were decimating the rain forests to capitalize on the world's demands for lumber. Political leaders were turning their backs to the environmental devastation at the cost of both rain forest and rural farmer. One source stated that hired killings of human rights advocates, environmentalists, and farmers at that time accounted for one third of the deaths in the region. Dorothy wrote in her journal: "I don't want to flee, nor do I want to abandon these farmers who live without any protection in the forest. They have the sacrosanct right to aspire to a better life on land where they can live and work with dignity while respecting the environment."

On February 12, 2005, two gunmen followed Dorothy as she walked in an isolated rural area to meet with peasant workers. As the gunmen approached, they asked Dorothy if she was carrying a weapon. "The only weapon I have is the Bible," she said. She pulled it from her bag and began to read from the Beatitudes: "Blessed are those who hunger and thirst for justice. . . " The gunmen fired six shots into her body, and she fell to her death on the dirt path.

Dorothy's death was not in vain. After she died, the Brazilian president placed under federal environmental protection nearly 20,000 square miles of the Amazon Basin in the region that had been Dorothy's home.[5]

In my four decades of ministry at Ginghamsburg Church, I have had countless opportunities to witness our church family members serving the kingdom of God in extraordinary ways, setting aside their own preferences and privileges to emulate the God of the towel. In some cases, entire families have made tremendous sacrifices. One of those families is the Garretts.

Jim and Rosie Garrett, parents of twin daughters Holly and Noel, are arguably our most contagious greeters in the children's ministry wing. No child can pass by Jim without a fist bump or high five, and you can literally see the disappointment in the kids' eyes any rare weekend that Jim and Rosie are not at their post. Both the Garretts are in their sixties, and Jim has had some issues with his back that now often have him at the door perched on a stool, but his contagious enthusiasm for loving on the kids has not diminished. Rosie too is a child-and-parent favorite. Whenever I pass by them on my weekend rounds, I have the reassuring feeling that all is right in God's universe.

Greeting is not the Garretts' only assignment. They serve as part of our guest services kitchen crew. Each week Jim and Rosie are in the kitchen prepping food, washing dishes, or delivering filled plates to guests at the weekly Wednesday Night Café in the Worship Center. In fact, any large church event that includes a menu will typically find Rosie and Jim in the kitchen. Jim, who is retired, can also be found on campus weekdays covering behind-the-scenes administrative tasks that are never applauded but are critical for ministry.

As much as I admire the Garretts for their servant hearts, what really demonstrates their obedience and sacrifice to the mission of Jesus is the way they have entrusted God with the lives of their daughters and only children, Holly and Noel. Holly and Noel's names well represent how Jim and Rosie cherish them as exceptional gifts from God. Both women are passionate followers of Jesus and are deeply prayerful. Both caught the "mission bug" as college students, going on multiple mission trips to uncomfortable places such as Haiti. In the early-to mid-2000s the twins were both on staff at Ginghamsburg, with Holly serving as the high school pastor and Noel as a much-loved member of our children's ministry staff team. Yet both sensed an even larger calling.

In 2005, Noel moved to the Czech Republic, a country freshly out from under Soviet Union rule and arguably the most atheistic on earth. Noel spent the next nine years on a different continent from her parents—a young, unmarried woman showing up daily to do the challenging work of sharing the good (but very foreign) news of Jesus Christ with Czech women, men, and children. After a decade, sensing that her call to the Czech people was coming to an end, Noel moved to Ethiopia for a season and next transitioned to South Sudan. South Sudan was the newest country on earth, but it was experiencing the age-old problems so prevalent in Africa: tribalism, unrest, and government corruption. Noel was posted in Yei, South Sudan, as the church's emissary to our Imagine No Malaria project investments.

Noel's safety and provision were never a "sure bet" during her tenure in Yei.

A few years after Noel moved to the Czech Republic, twin sister Holly felt the call to Ethiopia. Holly has been teaching and ministering in Addis Ababa since 2011, largely apart from her family except for the brief period of time that Noel was posted in Addis as well.

In the summer of 2015, Noel returned to the states and is now leading Ginghamsburg's mission initiatives, still as a missionary who raises her own support. Holly remains in Ethiopia.

As a parent, I can only imagine how difficult it must have been over the years for Jim and Rosie to trust Jesus with their most precious treasure, their daughters. Many of us see our kids move away as adults to new places, and we miss them. But few of us know what it's like to release our children half a planet away into difficult and even dangerous places. Yet Jim has never lost the twinkle in his eye, and Rosie has never lost her smile. I look forward each day to the Scripture that Rosie faithfully prays in her quiet time and then posts on Facebook to encourage others before heading to work.

Wow! When I look at the Garretts, I see the God of the towel in the flesh. The Garretts are ordinary people making daily, extraordinary sacrifices on behalf of God's kingdom.

Jesus asked his disciples James and John if they really understood what they were signing up for: "Are you able to drink the cup that I am about to drink?" (Matthew 20:22 NRSV). The lifestyle of the Jesus follower comes with inherent risks: "Whoever wants to be my disciple must deny themselves and take up their cross daily and follow me. For whoever wants to save their life will lose it, but whoever loses their life for me will save it" (Luke 9:23-24).

Jesus calls each of us to leave the confines of easy belief and institutional religion to risk a down-to-earth lifestyle of sacrificial love.

DEFINING GREATNESS

At some point during the Advent-Christmas season, we usually read the following text from the Book of Isaiah:

> For to us a child is born, / to us a son is given, / and the government will be on his shoulders. / And he will be called / Wonderful Counselor, Mighty God, / Everlasting Father, Prince of Peace. / Of the greatness of his government and peace / there will be no end. / He will reign on David's throne / and over his kingdom, / establishing and upholding it with justice and righteousness from / that time on and forever. / The zeal of the LORD Almighty will accomplish this.
>
> (Isaiah 9:6-7)

The revelation of "Mighty God" through the birth, life, death, and resurrection of Jesus turns all worldly ideas of power and greatness on their head. Jesus reveals a God who is for the underdog. Did you notice that the very first announcement of Jesus' birth (described in Luke 2:8-20) was made to shepherds and not to political or religious leaders? At the time of Jesus' birth, rabbis considered shepherds to be religious outcasts.

Later in Isaiah, we read more about how God shows up on behalf of the outcast: "A bruised reed he will not break, / and a smoldering wick he will not snuff out" (Isaiah 42:3). In other words, God stands with us even in our fractured failures and singed setbacks. Who are the outcasts in our communities and throughout the world this Christmas? How can we as followers of Jesus demonstrate God's love in practical, need-meeting ways?

More often, it seems, we respond with fear. The Paris bombing attacks on the night of November 13, 2015, left 130 people dead and hundreds wounded; the attacks sent shockwaves of fear throughout the world. A short time later, there was a deadly assault on a San

Bernardino social services center by a U.S.-born Muslim man and his Pakistani wife; fear caused some with influential voices to call for banning entry of all Muslims to the U.S. Some voices within the church advocated the deportation of illegal immigrants while the immigrants' children would remain in the U.S., separated from their parents. The political debates of 2016 played on America's fear factor, which caused many to overlook God's commands to "love your enemies and pray for those who persecute you" (Matthew 5:44) and treat "the foreigner residing among you . . . as your native-born" and "love them as yourself" (Leviticus 19:33-34). As we are reminded in the First Letter of John, "Such love has no fear, because perfect love expels all fear" (4:18 NLT).

The frenzied pace of the contemporary Christmas season that includes buying gifts, hosting parties, cooking, and more can cause us to miss the most important gift: relationships. Our obsession with presents causes us to forfeit the gift of presence. Jesus was never too busy nor felt too important to stop and meet the needs of a blind beggar or welcome children to sit on his lap. It is always helpful for me to remember during this, one of the busiest seasons in the life of a pastor's family, that *life is short and death is certain!* Let's all take time in this season of light and life to be fully present with those who are closest to our heart and those whom Jesus brings into our life path.

The frenzied pace of the contemporary Christmas season that includes buying gifts, hosting parties, cooking, and more can cause us to miss the most important gift: relationships.

Jesus demonstrated that leadership means being elevated in influence by being lowered to the place of greatest need. In the kingdom of God, increased responsibility will always mean decreased privilege.

My co-author for *Down to Earth* is a prime example of what this may look like. Rachel Billups joined our staff team more than two years ago from Cincinnati, where she was lead pastor of a multi-site church. In her role at Ginghamsburg as Executive Pastor of Discipleship, Rachel has taken on an expansive span of care, bringing leadership to our Tipp City Campus discipleship, worship, missions, and family ministries for all ages. She also brings the word at our five weekend worship celebrations at least fifteen to twenty times each year, sometimes alternating between our two urban campuses to preach for a weekend.

It's a big job, and it grows even bigger considering that she and her husband, Jon, manage two careers and three young children. Jon is a public schoolteacher and a football coach. It's a delicate balance for the family in summers and falls as Rachel prepares ministries for the start of a new discipleship year and Jon is busy on the football practice and game fields. Jon has sacrificed his employment a number of times through the years of their marriage as Rachel attended seminary and moved through multiple pastoral appointments.

Rachel knows what it's like to have tremendous leadership responsibility while never losing the understanding of what it means to be a servant. She and Jon work hard to make sure their kids always feel loved and supported, and Rachel is also exceptionally diligent to support her ministry teams' events, meet one-on-one with church family members, write and send personalized prayers to those who need encouragement, deliver meaningful sermons, and oversee the myriad administrative details that make ministry and mission happen. She is also on the sidelines of as many of her husband's football games as she can attend, given her commitments as pastor.

One of my favorite servant ministries that Rachel and Jon use to serve others is the every-other-Thursday "Open Table" event that Rachel mentioned in the previous chapter. Talk about radical hospitality! Most people would be completely intimidated to host

too much!

dinner at their own table without knowing who or how many will show up. Of course, there is also the expense and stress of providing at least part of the menu at each gathering. Open Table invites all people to come as they are, and they do. This ministry vividly illustrates the definition of "greatness" and down-to-earth servant leadership.

I AM SENDING YOU

Sometimes I believe we confuse the second coming of Christ with the first. We jump right to the Book of Revelation to see Christ return as the victorious king, judging the world and establishing a new heaven on earth; and we forget that we are still living in the reality of the first coming, when God's Son arrived on Planet Earth not as victor but as victim. He came as a baby, thrust into the experience of an oppressed refugee; and as Savior and suffering servant, Jesus continues to show up in the world's places of pain. We have a God who identifies with the slave chained in the hold of a ship, the Jewish prisoner in Auschwitz, the sick child shivering with malaria in South Sudan, and the soaked Syrian refugee family anxiously clinging to rescuers as they clamber out of a collapsing boat along Greece's shoreline.

We like to focus on the miracle of the Resurrection, but frankly, resurrection is not a big deal for the God who created the universe. Anyway, Jesus wasn't the first person to be resurrected; remember Lazarus, as well as a few others along the way? To me, the greatest miracle is not the Resurrection, but the Incarnation, when God took human form. That's scandalous love!

In light of all the atrocities going on in the world around us, many of us ask ourselves, "Where is God?" We often say, "Somebody ought to do something about that." Well, let me tell you: God has come to do something about it, and you are the somebody he is going to do it through! Jesus said, "As the Father sent me, so I am sending you" (John 20:21 CEB).

You may be thinking, "God surely doesn't mean *me*. What could I do? It would only be a drop in the bucket at best." That's another great strategy on the part of darkness. Evil will always try to convince us that we are powerless, that we can't change anything. But Jesus says we have full access to the unlimited resources of God, to "rivers of living water" (John 7:38). As Jesus followers, the word *can't* should not be allowed in our vocabulary.

You have heard it said that the only thing necessary for evil to succeed is for good people to do nothing, and it's true. We have been the recipients of God's scandalous love; now we must go and live it out actively on behalf of others.[6]

THE GREATEST ACT OF SERVICE

Christmas, along with Easter, marks one of two seasons each year when our friends, family members, and neighbors are most spiritually open. This means that Advent is one of our best opportunities to perform the greatest act of service that anyone could ever commit: introducing another person into a life-giving and life-transforming relationship with Jesus Christ. This past Advent season, I was sad but honored to be part of the end-of-life celebration for the son of Steve, one of my high school friends. Although the circumstances of my reconnection with Steve were unfortunate, it did remind me of a key role Steve had played in pointing me toward Jesus.

Steve and I grew up in the same church together. In high school I liked and looked up to Steve, who is a year older than I am; though if I am completely honest, I would have to say that part of what I liked the most about Steve was that he already had a car and a driver's license. Far from being a strong student, I seemed to experience one troubling incident after another, leaving my parents frustrated. One of the few people who didn't give up on me during that time was Steve, even though he had nothing to gain and much to lose by hanging out with me.

After one of my escapades, Steve approached me and said, "Mike, I want you to go to youth group with me tonight." I'm not sure exactly how I replied, but I'm sure my response started out with something resembling, "No way! I'm not going to some stupid youth group. That's not what I'm into." Steve, however, refused to take no for an answer. He didn't give me an out, even pulling up at the curb outside my house that evening to give me a ride. Now Steve, by himself, could not change my life, but he could persistently keep trying to introduce me to the Someone who could. If it weren't for the Steves in my life, I would never have written this book or spent nearly forty years as a local church pastor, firmly committed to knowing nothing "except Jesus Christ and him crucified" (1 Corinthians 2:2).

Friends don't let friends miss out on the Kingdom. Inviting others to meet Jesus is our most sacred task, and Christmas is the perfect opportunity to include others.

Friends don't let friends miss out on the Kingdom. Inviting others to meet Jesus is our most sacred task, and Christmas is the perfect opportunity to include others, inviting them to pull up a chair at the Kingdom table. I recognize that "inviting" for many of us can be personally challenging. We all have excuses: *I don't know the Bible. I'm too shy. It won't work anyway.* In those moments of fear, we have to remember that we are not called or expected to change anyone's life. We are merely asked to share our own story of life transformation and offer an opportunity. The rest belongs to Christ.

As Rachel will discuss in the next chapter, Jesus' mother Mary was only a young teenager when she was approached by God's messenger about her incredible and personally dangerous mission to bear God's

Son. The responsibility was uncomfortable, inconvenient, and scary. Yet Mary responded, in essence, "I am your servant, Lord. Let it be done to me as you say" (Luke 1:38 paraphrase).

Let's make that our heart's desire and prayer this Advent as we demonstrate down-to-earth lifestyles that point others to Christ.

Reflection:
A Lifestyle of Service

When he had finished washing their feet, he put on his clothes and returned to his place. "Do you understand what I have done for you?" he asked them. "You call me 'Teacher' and 'Lord,' and rightly so, for that is what I am. Now that I, your Lord and Teacher, have washed your feet, you also should wash one another's feet."

(John 13:12-14)

I'm not afraid of washing feet. In fact, with two boys at home I've scrubbed my share of dirty toes. But footwashing may not have the same cultural relevance as it did in Jesus' day.

For Jesus, when he gathered with his disciples at the Last Supper, he first washed their feet. It seemed shocking and made the disciples uncomfortable, which may have been why Jesus did it. By washing their feet, he was calling them to do the same for each other. But of course his actions weren't about feet or even footwashing. They were visual reminders that as his followers, we are to be servants first, even if (or especially if) we are leaders in the church. So, what does footwashing look like in the twenty-first century? Maybe it's like More Than Carpenters.

I ran across a friend of mine one evening at a Kingdom Investors Meeting, a gathering time for church leaders who invest their time and resources into the movement we call Ginghamsburg Church. That night I learned that my friend was part of a group called More Than Carpenters, a ministry started by people who wanted to use carpentry, plumbing, welding, and other gifts to serve people inside the church and throughout the community. The ministry had taken a while to get off the ground. Even though the members had possessed the resources of skill and time (many were retired), their ministry was just not taking shape.

But then something happened. The ministry leader, Doug Powell, read a book called *When Helping Hurts*, by Steve Corbett and Brian Fikkert, and realized that if their ministry was to help the community, it could not be merely a handout, but a hand up. With this in mind, Doug and his group established some criteria—each person they helped had to contribute to the project. Sometimes the contribution was financial; other times, the person bought materials for someone else—a new wheelchair ramp for an elderly woman, a new drain for someone's sink.

It also meant an invitation to participate in the work. Instead of simply doing work for others, the men and women in More Than Carpenters committed themselves to teaching individuals and families the basics of plumbing, heating, carpentry, and anything else that would contribute a long-term solution to a short-term problem.

Finally, the group came to believe that Jesus was calling them to share God's good news—through praying with others, getting to know someone's story, and, if the opportunity arose, unapologetically inviting these persons into a saving relationship with Jesus Christ. The new framework changed everything. Before, they were struggling to get their ministry off the ground; now more than fifty people are serving the community through their More Than Carpenters ministry. These men and women are using the gifts of their hands, bringing resources to people who are in need of their gifts and, in turn, teaching the community about our interdependence with one another.

They have learned that service is more than a one-time act. It is more than projects. Service is a way of life.

Jesus used a bowl of water and a towel to serve his disciples. What gifts can you use this Advent season to serve the people around you?

Servant God, continue to remind us of your simple acts of love and service. Throughout Advent, help us to carve time out of our schedules to serve the people in our homes, churches, and communities. In Jesus' name. Amen.

From *Down to Earth: Devotions for the Season*
by Rachel Billups. Abingdon Press, 2016.

4.

Down to Earth
Obedience

4.

Down to Earth Obedience

Rachel

Therefore, my dear friends, as you have always obeyed—not only in my presence, but now much more in my absence— continue to work out your salvation with fear and trembling, for it is God who works in you to will and to act in order to fulfill his good purpose. (Philippians 2:12-13)

After writing the beautiful words above to the Jesus followers in Philippi, Paul reminded the Philippians that they already knew what they were supposed to do. Paul, and really Jesus, was calling them to live a life of obedience.

REDEFINING OBEDIENCE

Obedience is not my favorite word. It's a hard word for me, perhaps because I have an inner struggle against authority. I like to be in charge of my own life, and the word, oddly, makes me feel a little out of control. Also, when I hear the word I am transported back to my childhood. Growing up, there were all kinds of rules, most of which were designed for the safety of me and my siblings, such as "Don't go wandering in the woods alone."

Other rules were simply common sense, such as "Don't play baseball in the living room." But sure enough, when the weather was bad or too hot to go outside, we created makeshift bases right there in our tiny living room and played baseball. I can't count the number of times we broke the glass figurines that were stationed on a shelf above first base. (If you go to my mom's house today, those figurines are still on that same shelf, cracks and all.) It was a good rule, but we did not follow it.

Playing baseball led to broken figurines and, at times, bloody noses. My mom—like the mother in the movie *A Christmas Story* who declared, "You're going to shoot your eye out!"—was constantly shouting warnings, which we might or might not heed. My brother, sister, and I often found ourselves struggling with obedience, and it did not stop with baseball. As we grew, the rules became "Don't stay out past your curfew," "Don't drink," and "Don't smoke." (That was my brother—never, ever me.) Don't, don't, and don't. As I grew, I came to believe that obedience was just a way to avoid punishment, and I should practice just enough obedience to avoid getting into trouble.

What about you? Maybe hearing the word *obedience* does not transport you back to your parents' home, but it might make you think of a bad experience at elementary school, or getting yelled at on the bus, or being on the receiving end of a scolding from an elderly lady in the neighborhood. Whatever negative feeling the word conjures up in your mind, sometimes it's difficult to relate obedience to following Jesus. Many times at church, we heard *Thou shalt not* more than we heard about the grace of Jesus, creating the belief for some of us that religion or faith is mostly about strict obedience or adherence to a set of rules and regulations.

Obedience needs to be redefined when it comes to faith in Jesus. It's not about punishment; it's about saying a big *yes* to God.

I've heard several horror stories about people who have struggled with faith because of the rules and regulations force-fed to them at church or by "religious" parents. The rules and regulations become overwhelming, and those folks turn away from faith. Also, much like my experience with obeying my parents, when we attempt to equate Christianity with a set of rules and regulations that are supposed to be obeyed, we make obedience more about avoiding trouble than about living fully into the faith that comes from being a follower of Jesus.

That definition of obedience lends itself to fear rather than faith. Obedience needs to be redefined when it comes to faith in Jesus. It's not about punishment; it's about saying a big *yes* to God.

A BIG YES

How do we redefine our perception of obedience? When I am looking to erase a false spiritual definition that has been embedded in my mind about God and the way God works in the world, I go to the Bible. Maybe I'm stubborn or dense, but it's not enough for me just to hear about it; I need to see it. A beautiful example of a big *yes* is found in the story of Mary, Jesus' mother.

Mary was a teenager when a messenger of God visited her. I can imagine that she was doing what most teenage girls in the first century might have been doing—sewing, planting, preparing meals, contributing to the family economy in any way she could. Mary's family was not wealthy. They were simple people, perhaps even what we would consider poor people, and she was doing what she could to help the family survive.

As different as Mary's life seems from the lives of modern teenagers—she certainly did not have the electronic and social media distractions of the twenty-first century—there may actually have been some strong similarities. Many teenagers in our communities are striving to help their families stay together, perhaps navigating the rough relationships of the parents. Some are working extra jobs to help pay the bills, and some are dodging friends' or family members' addictions. They experience daily stress. In a *Huffington Post* article, "American Teens Are Even More Stressed Than Adults," writer Carolyn Gregoire stated, "Even before the pressure of work and adulthood set in, for most young Americans, stress has become a fact of daily life."[1] Today's teens are navigating an ever-increasing amount of pressure, workload, and depression. The stress that teens feel is not some special stress of adolescence; it is similar to the stress and pressure felt by adults. In some cases, the adults in their lives are actually the cause of their stress, as teens feel the pressure of attempting to help the adults in their lives survive and thrive.

Even though Mary and modern teens are separated by thousands of years, I can imagine Mary's struggle as being, similarly, a struggle for survival. It was in the middle of this struggle to survive that Mary was visited by an angel—a messenger from God. The messenger brought Mary news that she was going to be a pregnant, unwed teenager. In our Christmas pageants and plays we declare it good news; but in fact, for Mary the messenger's news was hard news, scary news, and news that was difficult to receive.

One does not have to be a teenager to know the sinking feeling that accompanies this kind of unwelcome news. Throughout our churches, communities, and neighborhoods, people are receiving news today that is causing fear and confusion—a medical diagnosis, a pink slip, divorce papers in the mail, a note from a teacher, a call that a loved one has died. It was in this state of fear and confusion that we find Mary. This is the Mary we discover in Luke 1, a real-life teenager in the midst of deeply challenging and stressful circumstances.

Sometimes we want to rush ahead in Scripture and get to the good parts of Mary's story, failing to observe that obedience is not learned when our lives are comfortable or easy; obedience is forged in the middle of the mess.

In the middle of Mary's mess, she realized God was asking her a question: "Mary, will you be obedient? Will you say *yes*?" That moment for Mary was not about avoiding punishment. Rather, it provided the opportunity for Mary to say a big *yes* to God. Could God see beyond Mary's situation? Could God see all the possibilities for Mary's life? Could God see a miracle waiting to be birthed? Absolutely, God could and did see the divine possibilities for Mary's future. But all Mary could see was what was right in front of her.

Unwed, poor, uneducated, unimportant, insignificant, soon to be rejected by her family and community, Mary did not face an easy yes. Yet when asked the life-bending question, Mary chose obedience. Mary said, *"Yes!"*

> "I am the Lord's servant," Mary answered. "May your word to me be fulfilled." Then the angel left her.
>
> (Luke 1:38)

Like Mary, some of us today find ourselves struggling. Like Mary, our lives might be a little scandalous. Like Mary, we may be scared out of our minds and not know what to do next. The first step is to ask ourselves, "Right here and right now, what would it mean for me to say yes to God? What is my big yes?"

Throughout each Christmas and Advent season there are many things competing for our yes. What would it look like to give that yes to the people around us who need it most?

Maybe you need to say yes to your marriage; maybe for years you have said to yourself, "If he would only do this, or if she would only do that." Maybe you've hesitated to fully invest yourself or your love in your spouse. Maybe today is the day you'll finally make that commitment. Obedience—the big yes—means refraining from playing the "if/when" game. If she does this, if he does that, when he does this, when she does that. Today that game ends, and you say *yes* to your spouse.

Maybe you're navigating the drama of grown children over the holidays. You have allowed yourself to be pushed and pulled in all sort of directions, and today you are going to say *yes* to healthy boundaries, even if it means saying no to your own kids. Or you might be filled with resentment about work. Finding joy and commitment in the workplace can be difficult. But today you can say *yes* to a new attitude. You may feel you are drowning financially with no foreseeable end in sight, or maybe your self-esteem is in the toilet. You may find yourself struggling with a chronic illness. It may never go away, and so today your *yes* means accepting God's grace to endure the pain.

Regardless of what you're facing, obedience is more than simply wishing for circumstances to change. Obedience is not a half-hearted, "Well, God, maybe you can help me out." Obedience means believing that God can do a miracle in our lives and then aligning ourselves with what God wants, not what we want.

Obedience is not a hazy mental exercise. It's not "Someday when God asks me to do something big, I'll consider it." It means an out-of-control, doesn't-feel-right, maybe-it-might, how-can-this-be... *Yes!*

So, how do we say learn to say yes?

THE PATH TO OBEDIENCE

Paul gave the Jesus followers at Philippi—and us—a path to yes. Like any path, it has several steps. The first step is to remember.

Therefore, my dear friends, as you have always obeyed—not only in my presence, but now much more in my absence—continue to work out your salvation with fear and trembling. (Philippians 2:12)

For Christians, Advent marks the beginning of the liturgical year. As people of faith we need regular reminders of what has happened in the past: both our collective past and our personal past.

Collectively we have a history, God's salvation history. That history declares that God has been, God is, and God will be good and faithful. Mary was privy to the collective memory of her people—a memory proclaiming that the God of Abraham, Isaac, and Jacob had delivered God's people out of the arms of their oppressors.

The LORD said, "I have indeed seen the misery of my people in Egypt. I have heard them crying out because of their slave drivers, and I am concerned about their suffering. So I have come down to rescue them from the hand of the Egyptians and to bring them up out of that land into a good and spacious land, a land flowing with milk and honey—the home of the Canaanites, Hittites, Amorites, Perizzites, Hivites and Jebusites."

(Exodus 3:7-8)

When Mary's people were being taxed and continually oppressed by their Roman oppressors, Mary remembered the words of her people and the promises of her God. That was their collective memory.

Each Advent, Jesus followers remember our story, a story of deliverance and rescue by God. But God, instead of saving a specific nation, rescues the whole wide world through the birth of God's Son. At Advent, we remind each other of God's work in and through God's people. If the Bible were just another printed book, it could be perceived as stale or viewed simply as a collection of children's stories. Yet through the power of the Holy Spirit, the Bible leads us to the

Living Word Jesus Christ, and the past and present memory of God's grace and presence that came to Planet Earth is birthed in us anew. The pull and push of fear, confusion, pressure, and stress in our lives attempts to distract us with a different story. But with some reflection this Advent, each one of us can rediscover in our lives the powerful moments of God's grace, goodness, and provision.

Even we preacher types tend to have moments when we forget God's grace. When others' expectations of me butt up against the limits of my perceived ability or capacity, I can find myself in a state of fear and paralysis. Sometimes when people ask me to do things that I believe are beyond my capacity, my initial reaction is "No way!" or "What if I can't finish the task?" or "What if I don't meet your expectations?" In those moments, I'm tempted to give up or give in, whether the demands are at work, at home, with family, with friends, or about the ever-growing expectation of the holidays. It might sound silly, but in that frame of mind the littlest things can send me over the edge, such as the sugar cookies I promised to bake for my kids' Christmas party! Those are the moments when I need to remember: I can do this because God has been, God is, and God will be good and faithful.

As Paul described in his letter to the Philippians, the first step on the path to yes is to remember. The second step is to trust, "for it is God who works in you to will and to act in order to fulfill his good purpose" (Philippians 2:13).

We have to trust that God is working on our behalf, for our good and the good of those around us. Of course, saying we trust God is one thing, but living out that trust is a very different matter. I will not pretend that it's easy to have faith, to believe, to live a life based on a person and a God we cannot see with our own two eyes. Sometimes we dabble in trusting God; we treat God as if we are just casually dating: "Hey, God, let's see how it goes. I like you, I know you like me; let's be friends and just see if this works out." We trust God as long as everything is smooth, good, simple, and right in our life. But then the minute things get tough, life becomes rocky, something does not go our way, when things get hard, we bail. But this is not a casual dating relationship; a yes to God is deeper than that.

If there is a relational picture of saying yes, the picture is marriage. When two people are united in marriage they make promises. They say yes "for better, for worse, for richer, for poorer, in sickness and in health, till death do us part." This is an obedient yes. When things are hard—when the kids are sick, when life gets routine, when you look at the stranger next to you in bed and say, "Who are you?"—that's when our promise is tested and our yes comes into question. It is messy! So is our relationship with God. At the beginning it is new—butterflies, rainbows, and sweet parades. But as life gets difficult, as we harden, then trust begins to fade. It is in the middle of the mess when we must say yes, not just once but again and again; it's what Paul is referring to when he calls for the Philippians to "continue to work out your salvation." Trust seems easy when everything is smooth in our lives; but when we, like Mary, are standing face-to-face with a message we don't want to hear, trusting God is anything but easy.

This past Advent season, I journeyed with so many people who had heard things they did not want to hear: parents who were told their newborn was not going to survive, a young mom who received news that the cancer was back, spouses who had been told, "I want out because I don't love you anymore." These are some of the darkest moments of life; they are a real mess. It's in these moments that our trust is tested. So how do we know whether we still trust God?

The truest test of trust is our attitude. Can you or I thank God even in the middle of the mess? I am not proposing "fake it till you make it" theology or putting on a happy face even though we are dying on the inside. Faith-filled folk need to be find a balance between authentically, honestly revealing what it means to be genuinely human in moments of suffering and "bleeding" all over the place so that others are overwhelmed by our wounds.

An attitude of gratitude is called for during the good, the bad, and the in-between. I have to confess that I am still working on gratitude. Sometimes I say out loud to God (and frankly to anyone one else who is listening), "I didn't sign up for this!" But then I'm reminded that I have a choice. I can choose a crappy attitude that results in bitterness, anger, and resentfulness. (Honestly, there are some days when I feel justified in choosing crappy.) Or I can choose to be thankful.

Paul reminded the Jesus-following folk at Philippi that God had begun a work in them, a work of the Holy Spirit moving in the lives of very ordinary, down-to-earth people. When we who are ordinary say thank you, we give God space in our hearts, minds, and souls to do a new work in us. "Thank you" gives me a glimpse of God's glorious light in my life, penetrating the darkness that so often creeps in.

It's through gratitude that we lay open our hearts for God to do some major surgery—cutting away the anger, bitterness, and resentfulness while pouring God's Spirit into our hearts!

Ann Voskamp, author of *One Thousand Gifts*, said, "And when I give thanks for the seemingly microscopic, I make a place for God to grow within me."[2] It's through gratitude that we lay open our hearts for God to do some major surgery—cutting away the anger, bitterness, and resentfulness while pouring God's Spirit into our hearts! Without gratitude there is no trust, just as without power your latest smartphone is nothing more than a paperweight. Even if you don't believe in your spouse, your doctor, your trainer, your banker, your friend, your teacher, or even yourself, once you express gratitude you are saying, "But I do believe in God." It is impossible to feel truly grateful and then go back on our yes to God.

Mary was grateful, even though her life situation did not become easy or comfortable. Using the words that we know as the Magnificat, Mary more than declared her thank-you; she sang it.

> "My soul glorifies the Lord
> and my spirit rejoices in God my Savior,
> for he has been mindful
> of the humble state of his servant.
> From now on all generations will call me blessed,
> for the Mighty One has done great things for me—
> holy is his name." (Luke 1:46-49)

This was Mary's song of thanksgiving in the face of community rejection. In a culture of honor and shame, her song to God would have brought shame to Mary's life, and yet she chose to say yes, actively naming God's new reality. This new reality was more than personal; it was not just for Mary. It was also for the people around her. Mary did not fully trust until she was able to thank God for her whole situation.

Pause for a moment. What is happening in your life right now? Do you struggle to maintain an attitude of gratitude? Can you stop gritting your teeth long enough to surrender, knowing that God can use even what you are going through to create healing space in your life? Do you trust? Do you believe God is big enough and small enough to birth a miracle in your life?

This is not about pretending that the bad, the scary, and the unfortunate are good. It's about recognizing that in the middle of it all, God is good; and because God is good, God can be trusted and praised.

LIGHT INTO DARKNESS

God wants to do a work in us and through us, not merely so that we can have some warm, fuzzy feeling toward God, but so that we can be God's truth on display. In other words, our yes is not merely for us.

Our yes cannot be hoarded or placed on a shelf. Our yes is an act of obedience to be shared with the entire world. After all, Mary's yes did not change only Mary's life but all of our lives. She was not kidding when she declared that through this one miracle God was changing everything for her and for her people. God was and is delivering and rescuing the whole wide world through the birth of a baby—God with us, God in the flesh, God traveling down to earth. As simple as your own act of obedience might be, your yes has the power to change you and the people around you.

Now, I certainly don't want to place too much weight on an everyday yes, because it can be debilitating. We can become paralyzed, afraid of making the wrong choice. That's not the point. I simply want us to recognize the power of a simple yes. Paul understood that power. It was why he wrote,

> Do everything without grumbling or arguing, so that you may become blameless and pure, "children of God without fault in a warped and crooked generation." Then you will shine among them like stars in the sky. (Philippians 2:14-15)

We are called to be light in what sometimes seems an ever-present darkness: wars, division, anger, hatred—the list goes on and on. Jesus reminded us,

> "You are the light of the world. A town built on a hill cannot be hidden. Neither do people light a lamp and put it under a bowl. Instead they put it on its stand, and it gives light to everyone in the house."
> (Matthew 5:14-15)

I believe this world is waiting for some light—light that will not appear magically in the sky but will shine and is shining through you. That light comes through obedience. The world is waiting for your light. People want to see it, to experience it, to know it's possible to live a life of obedience to God. The world is saying, "Let's see your big *yes!*"

In Chapter 1, I reminded you that down-to-earth people don't focus on arguments, differences, or red cups. We are a people who refuse to allow our differences to create hatred between us. In Philippians 2, Paul had to remind the Jesus followers at Philippi that there was no room for bickering and second guessing when we are called to take our yes into the world. Our yes does not add to the noise, the chaos, the hate, the frustration. Folk do not want us to add to the divisive nature of the global conversation; they want us, through our yes, to become a breath of fresh air for the world.

A Breath of Fresh Air

That's what we are called to be for one another and for the world: a breath of fresh air. When people experience followers of Jesus, they are supposed to walk away feeling lighter, happier, healthier, and frankly changed; not confused, frustrated, judged, or angry.

I'm the kind of person who loves to meet strangers on airplanes. My colleagues, including my coauthor on this book, poke fun at me because when I travel on a plane with them, they always observe me making a fast friend of the unfamiliar person seated next to me. In those conversations, inevitably I will be asked the dreaded question, "What do you do?" I have learned over the years that I can make something up like "product manager for a small business," or I can ask them to guess. No one ever guesses what I do for a living. But when I tell them I am a pastor, it often will open the door to spiritual conversation.

What I have discovered is that most folk, even if they have no faith, will gladly hold a healthy conversation about faith and spirituality. People want to talk about it. They want to discuss what it means not merely to believe in God but to lead a life worth living. They do not like being preached at; they want to enter the conversation on their own terms. And in my experience they are hungry to see God's love and light on display in a real, live human being. They don't want just concepts; they're looking for less talk and more action.

Paul wrote that as children of God we would shine like stars, not because there is something extraordinary about us but because God's Spirit is alive and pouring out of us. God's love and light are contagious.

Several months ago I was hanging out at a local coffee shop called Warehouse 4, trying to make progress on some work projects without the distractions of the office. Warehouse 4 might as well be an annex of Ginghamsburg Church; our staff members spend a lot of time there. While plugging away on my computer, I noticed a group of women at a nearby table. They appeared to be older than I was—more seasoned, if you will—and I could tell they were friends. I tried to mind my own business and not eavesdrop, but I couldn't help myself. These women were not gossiping; they were not complaining about their struggles. Instead, they were laughing, sharing, grieving, and caring for one another. Even though they had been through a lot—cancer, the loss of a spouse, challenges with adult children—God's light was radiating from them. They were a joy to watch. It took everything inside me not to go over and join their conversation!

I continued to work. Soon they cleared their table and one by one headed out to their various destinations. As the last of the group walked toward the door, with hesitation I stopped her and said, "I need you to know that you and your friends were a real gift! I loved seeing how you love one another so well!" She looked at me with a smile in her eyes and said, "Aren't joy and laughter contagious!" After she left, I thought to myself: that's what it means to shine like stars. That day I glimpsed people shining, not by grumbling or arguing or focusing attention on themselves, but by using their yes to bring light and joy to the people around them. I saw in those women a big yes, a contagious yes, a yes that I wanted to be a part of. It wasn't because they were cool or young or hip, but because I could feel God's love flowing in and through them.

I wonder, what is your big *yes* as you travel the path to Christmas? What is God asking you to do?

This past Advent, my father-in-law wanted to retire but was unsure of his financial future. The changes being made by his employer were resulting in an increasingly stressful workload. As my husband and I watched my in-laws wrestle with this decision, we asked ourselves, "Could we offer space in our home for this season of our lives? Could we share our house and our space?"

This form of sharing felt like an act of obedience. We prayed, wrestled, debated, and finally made the genuine offer to extend our table and share our home. It was the first Christmas that we gathered together as an extended family around the dinner table. I suspect that I am not alone. You may find yourself sharing your life and home this Christmas, whether it involves caring for a child or grandchild, helping with an aging parent, or opening your home to a person who is unrelated.

Obedience means saying yes and then stepping into the future that God has for us and the people around us.

Obedience comes in all kinds of forms. It may mean sacrificially giving up our visions of the perfect North American Christmas to invest in a struggling community halfway across the globe. It may mean sharing our lives and our Christmas with people from neighborhoods we would not dream of living in. We don't do these things out of obligation or duty; after all, God isn't holding our lives up against some kind of spiritual measuring stick or totaling up our good deeds for the year. Obedience means saying yes and then stepping into the future that God has for us and the people around us. A yes to God may mean deepening our relationships, maintaining gratitude in the midst of chronic pain, living out a new way to navigate our workplaces, embodying a healthy self-image, serving the needs of our families and friends, or simply trusting our future to God.

Mary, standing face-to-face with a messenger from God, did not try to avoid trouble or pain. Honestly, I wonder if she could even fathom what God was asking her to do. Chances are, all she saw was what was right in front of her—confusion, fear, pregnancy, a fiancé who might not understand; but also joy, anticipation, and wondrous possibilities.

> "I am the Lord's servant," Mary answered. "May your word to me be fulfilled." (Luke 1:38)

Mary said yes. She truly was an obedient servant. This Advent, will we choose to be obedient servants?

I invite you to pray this prayer with me...

If you've ever assumed you're too old for anyone to listen to your wisdom...

If you think you're too young for people to care about your dreams...

If you imagine you have too many problems for anyone to listen to...

If you've labeled yourself too far gone for God to want you...

Then let these words wash over you.

Jesus, you came down to earth and moved right into our neighborhood; you became one of us. You did not come so we could pretend to be super-spiritual or superhuman but so your light and love could shine in and through us. Light of the World, shine in the darkest places of our hearts, shine where fear and confusion have left us paralyzed and unable to move forward, shine when we are face-to-face with the question of obedience. Jesus, this Advent and Christmas may we offer to you our simple yes, and may that yes ignite a change in us and in those around us. Give us the grace to shine like stars in the sky so that we will carry your light and love into the world. In your powerful name, Jesus Christ our Lord. Amen.

Reflection: Driving Without a Bumper

Therefore, my dear friends, as you have always obeyed—not only in my presence, but now much more in my absence—continue to work out your salvation with fear and trembling, for it is God who works in you to will and to act in order to fulfill his good purpose.

(Philippians 2:12-13)

One icy, snowy Saturday afternoon, I was hanging out at home with my best friend, Sarah. We had just watched *The Breakfast Club* and were determined to return the movie on time. (This was before the days of Redbox and Netflix.) My mom wasn't home, so I called to tell her we'd be venturing out into the winter weather. She told me in no uncertain terms to stay off the icy roads.

Now, I was a young driver but not a new driver, and I deemed myself perfectly capable of navigating the icy roadways in order to avoid paying the late fee. I figured that if I was careful, we could return the movie and my mother would never be the wiser.

So, Sarah and I piled into my dirty turquoise 1996 Dodge Shadow. Oh, did I mention that we lived in the Hocking Hills, a neighborhood with an elevation change of nearly one thousand feet between my house and the rental store?

As we drove through the falling snow, we slowed down to twenty-five miles an hour, just to be sure we'd make it to the rental store safely. One mile into the journey, the car began to slide off into a ditch. In what seemed like a slow motion movie—not *The Breakfast Club*—the car turned 180 degrees, slipped off the road, and landed with the back bumper in a snow bank. Sarah and I jumped from the car, ran around to see if there was any damage, and decided everything looked good.

Yes, I thought to myself, *there's still a chance I will not get caught.*

With no cell phone and no house in sight, we prayed that someone would come to our rescue and that it would not be anyone who knew my parents. In minutes, a neighbor stopped by and offered to drag us out of the ditch. He got a rope from his pickup truck, tied it to our front axle, and pulled us out. The car came out of the snow, but the bumper did not. In a matter of minutes it had frozen to the icy bank, and now we were forced to dig it out.

With the help of my neighbor we made it back home, put the car in the driveway, and confronted the fact that we would have to pay the late fee. Worse yet, I would be caught. Evidence of my disobedience lay crumpled next to the garage door. When my mom arrived home, I received my punishment: I had to drive that Dodge Shadow without a bumper until I could afford to pay five hundred dollars for a new one. It was a steep price tag for a young adult who had a limited income.

My parents wanted me to understand that obedience is not about avoiding punishment; rather, it's about saying *yes* to the right action. They forced me to experience the consequences of my poor choice.

Today I'm an adult, but often I wonder if I really learned that lesson. Sometimes I still think of obedience as avoiding punishment, rather than saying *yes* to the right action. As a result, I've carried home a lot of "bumpers."

Perhaps you've had similar experiences in your life. Maybe you're carrying around a few bumpers yourself. God wants to work in your life and mine so God's purpose can be filled in and through us.

So, when facing the icy roads of life, remember how ugly a car looks without a bumper.

Lord, obedience is not the avoidance of punishment, but an opportunity for you to fulfill your good purpose in us and through us. Help me say yes to obedience. In Jesus' name. Amen.

From *Down to Earth: Devotions for the Season*
by Rachel Billups. Abingdon Press, 2016.

Epilogue

Epilogue

Be Loved.
Do Love.

Mike

In the beginning was the Word, and the Word was with God, and the Word was God. He was with God in the beginning. Through him all things were made; without him nothing was made that has been made. In him was life, and that life was the light of all mankind. The light shines in the darkness, and the darkness has not overcome it... The true light that gives light to everyone was coming into the world. He was in the world, and though the world was made through him, the world did not recognize him. He came to that which was his own, but his own did not receive him. Yet to all who did receive him, to those who believed in his name, he gave the right to become children of God. (John 1:1-5, 9-12)

"Jesus loves me, this I know." How amazing that one of the most life-altering truths in the universe is so perfectly encapsulated in the first few words of a simple Sunday school song! "Jesus loves *me*." So powerful, and yet so difficult for us to embrace as we struggle with our sense of worthiness—or lack of it. John 3:16, arguably the most recognized and quoted verse in the New Testament, declares that Jesus came to earth because "God so loved the world"—the entire world, including each of us. We've read it, we've heard it, we've even sung it…but we continually struggle to believe it.

Before we can love like Jesus, walk in the humility of Jesus, practice the servant lifestyle of Jesus, or say our big yes of obedience to Jesus, we must accept the full significance of God's love. We must allow ourselves to *be* loved, so that in turn we will find ourselves compelled to *do* love. We must unwrap the greatest gift ever given by our down-to-earth God, accept it for ourselves, and then extend it through Christ to others.

ALL WE NEED IS…

Some years ago, preparing for the Christmas Eve worship celebrations at Ginghamsburg Church, we sent a video crew out to create a "Person on the Street" interview segment in which we asked, "What do you think is the greatest need in the world today?" The most frequently given answer was money. Even Christians can default to thinking that the world's greatest problems can best be solved by money. But if money were the solution, God would have sent an economist.

Demographic studies in the area of Tipp City, Ohio, where I live, have identified leisure, recreation, and entertainment as key needs in the lives of the people who live there. But God didn't send an entertainer. Many people point to the power of positive thinking. But God didn't send a motivational speaker.

What is our most pressing need? Education is important but not the greatest need; in fact, some of us just need to start practicing what we already know. Millions of people need food, but there is enough food in the world to feed everybody on the planet. The root problem is selfishness. Because of it, there is inadequate and inequitable distribution of food on Planet Earth.

God didn't send an economist, an entertainer, a motivational speaker, a teacher, or an agriculturist; God sent a Savior. What we most need is God!

God didn't send an economist, an entertainer, a motivational speaker, a teacher, or an agriculturist; God sent a Savior. What we most need is God!

Our religions don't go far enough. For most of us, "religion" means trying to do what we know we should be doing. Jesus did not come to bring religion. Scanning the news headlines each morning will quickly show us why religion is not the answer. In fact, it can be a major contributor to the world's most pressing problems. Religion can be legalistic, judgmental, and often, sadly, just plain ugly. It can be used as an excuse or cover-up for evil acts. Jesus did not come to bring religion; Jesus came as the Messiah to restore right relationships.

On the morning of Jesus' resurrection, as described in John 20, Mary Magdalene stood outside the tomb weeping, grief-stricken not only because of Jesus' crucifixion but because of her startling discovery that his body had disappeared. When Jesus first approached her, Mary did not recognize him. Jesus asked Mary in verse 15: "Woman, why are you crying? Who is it you are looking for?"

Note the word that Jesus used: Who—not what—are you looking for? Mary was seeking a body, but she had found the living Christ. We will never find what we are seeking in the "what," but only in a personal relationship with our down-to-earth Savior. Note also that Mary recognized Jesus in verse 16, after Jesus called her by her familiar name.

John 1:12 reassures us that "to all who did receive him, to those who believed in his name, he gave the right to become children of God." Yet, we often ignore the key point of John's assertion: we don't earn "beloved child" status based on merit. God loves you, not because you are good but because God is good. Jesus came so that we can learn to live into and under the inheritance we have as children of God. Jesus came so that we can fully embrace all the privileges and blessings of what it means to be God's children.

GOD ESTEEM

Being "born again" as Christians means discovering our true identity and being empowered to accept our full birthright as children of God. Too many of us have allowed our self-images to be shaped by other people. Their negative perceptions and statements about us at first wound us and then start to serve as fuel for the negative self-talk in our own lives. Maybe you've heard these statements: "You're not as smart as your sister." "You're overweight." "You're too skinny." Perhaps a coach told you, "You're not good enough to make the team." Some of us still struggle from the damage inflicted during our parents' rancorous divorces when we were kids. All these experiences help shape our self-image.

When I was an elementary school student in Cincinnati, Ohio, teachers determined our "potential" by first grade, and we were placed in groups based on that judgment. We would then remain with the same group all the way through high school. The categorizations were quite obvious. I imagine you can guess which students were in the A Group, the B Group, the C and D Groups. (Not very subtle, was it?) I don't know how naive they thought we were, but the administration didn't want to use the term F Group, so they called it the Z Group instead.

In first grade, the powers-that-be determined that my human potential was to be in the C Group, which was the lowest group you could be in and still take college preparatory courses in junior high and high school. C Group became my identity. Perhaps it's no wonder that I always struggled academically until I finished high school, at which time I was able to join my real group, "children of God." As a member of that group, I gained a new self-image by meeting Jesus and then went on to graduate magna cum laude from the University of Cincinnati.

Esteem issues for most kids have not improved since I was in grade school back in the 1950s. *The Huffington Post* has reported research revealing that twenty million women in the United States may be suffering from eating disorders: "By elementary school 40%-60% of girls say they worry about becoming too fat, a concern that once established stays with them for the rest of their lives."[1] It isn't just girls who have body-image issues. As *The New York Times* reported a few years ago, "Pediatricians are starting to sound alarm bells about boys who take unhealthy measures to try to achieve Charles Atlas bodies that only genetics can truly confer. Whether it is long hours in the gym, allowances blown on expensive supplements or even risky experiments with illegal steroids, the price American boys are willing to pay for the perfect body appears to be on the rise."[2]

Our nearly 24/7 obsession with social media does not help. Each day when I scroll through my Facebook news feed, I see results that people have posted from a steady diet of new quizzes for allegedly learning more about yourself. Simply enter your first name or birth date, select a number, and choose a picture from a group that most makes you feel a certain way; or note your favorite color or cartoon character, and receive a flattering analysis of the person you are. We can't wait to share the results and have fellow Facebook friends weigh in with affirmations. We are always looking for love in inadequate places.

As twenty-first-century Americans, we take repeated selfies, trying to capture just the right one to show how beautiful, silly, or talented we can be. We can sometimes go overboard in posting only the stories and photos that make our lives seem the most exciting. Conversely, we may go through seasons when we post photos of our wounds or "bleed out" our complete misery on the Internet. Don't get me wrong—I enjoy Facebook as much as the next person. I've been known to take a selfie or two, and online quizzes can be fun—if we don't take them too seriously. But if I have to resort to Facebook for my esteem, then it's an issue.

In 2015, *Forbes* was one of several publications to report on a study from the *Journal of Social and Clinical Psychology* finding that Facebook and depressive symptoms go hand-in-hand. The *Forbes* article noted that the key culprit in creating the linkage is social comparison—"that is, making comparisons, often between our most humdrum moments and our friends 'highlight reels'—the vacation montages and cute baby pics."[3]

In addition to public school experiences and social media habits, all kinds of factors can shape our identity. A friend who is about ten years younger than I am called recently and told me he was going through another divorce. This was his fifth marriage. He said, "I'm never going to get married again because I just don't have marriage potential; I can't be faithful."

I replied, "What do you mean you can't be faithful? Someone has lied to you. You are living below all the privileges and blessings of your inheritance as a child of God."

My friend responded, "No, Mike, when I came home from college and told my mom I was engaged, she said, 'You're not marriage material. Your daddy was a cheat, your grandfather was a cheat, it's in your blood.' "

I told my friend, "It's the Accuser who tells you those types of lies. Jesus came so you could fully live into all the rights and privileges of your inheritance in him."

KISSED BY THE PRINCE

Some of us have been caught in a shameful situation in our lives, whether inadvertently or because of poor choices. Others may be harboring dark secrets that we're trying to cover up, and we feel ashamed. Many of us have had our understanding of God distorted because of a religious encounter that left us feeling judged and condemned.

Whatever situation you find yourself in, Jesus didn't come down to earth to give us religion; Jesus came to restore right relationships, first and most importantly our relationship with God. Perhaps the best gift you can give yourself this Christmas is to accept that God accepts you!

Perhaps the best gift you can give yourself this Christmas is to accept that God accepts you!

In the story of *Snow White*, the beautiful princess ate the forbidden fruit and went to sleep. No one could wake her up, not even those seven vertically challenged people who loved and were loved by Snow White. When we neglect our relationship with God, we fall into a spiritual sleep. Only after the prince comes along and awakens us with a kiss are we able to know who we are, whose we are, and what we were created for.

Being awakened by Jesus, however, is not the end of the journey; it's the beginning. What happens if you wake up and yet spend the whole day in bed? That's not life and life abundantly. Staying in bed, inertia, and apathy can lead to depression, boredom, and sometimes even to bad religion. Bad religion focuses on what can be seen, judging our appearance and actions. Jesus awakens us to the unseen, to the love of the Father and the power of the Holy Spirit.

Once we wake up, we must resolve to rise and follow. Human beings are great procrastinators. We know what we should do, but we put off doing it. Think of the ancient magi, the three wise men of the Christmas story. Though popular depictions show the magi standing over Jesus' manger, we know that they didn't arrive until Jesus was two years old. It wasn't enough for them to know Jesus had been born; they wanted to witness the miracle. And so every day they had to make themselves get up and continue to follow God's star. I can only imagine the days when they found themselves in the middle of the desert and wondered, "What are we doing here?"

Before I was awakened by Jesus Christ, I was a classic underachiever. I was dealing with esteem issues. Frankly, I was kissing a lot of frogs! But Christ had a plan for my life, and he has one for yours. He told us and showed us that we have been created for a relationship with God and that God is like a parent. In the garden of Gethsemane, Jesus cried out to God the Father using the intimate name of *Abba*—"papa" or "daddy"—an almost childlike term that Palestinian children used for their father. The Apostle John wrote, "See what great love the Father has lavished on us, that we should be called children of God!" (1 John 3:1).

THE LOVE OF A FATHER

I love being a father and grandfather. Last Christmas morning my five grandchildren, ranging in age from one to six years old, discovered personalized stockings that my wife Carolyn and I had hung with care on our mantel. This year we will hang a sixth stocking for our newest grandson. We have always wanted our children to know the blessings, rights, and privileges that are available to them simply by being born into our household and that are available to our children's children as well. We want the coming generations to know there is nothing they could ever do that would separate them from our love. If this is how

I feel about my children in spite of my human insufficiency as a parent, how much more love must our heavenly Father lavish on us as his children?

As parents, we go out of our way to ensure that our kids never doubt our love. We work hard, sometimes holding down two or three jobs to provide for our kids. We want to be sure our four-year-old never has to ask when being tucked in at night, "Daddy, did you make the house payment this month?" or "Mommy, can I have clothes for school tomorrow?" This Christmas, we may even place presents under the tree that our kids really don't need or deserve. So, how much greater must be the love of our heavenly Father?

When my son, Jonathan, was growing up, our favorite times together were spent on sports, primarily on our shared love of baseball. I spent countless hours tossing pitches to Jonathan in the batting cage or in our backyard. My daughter, Kristen, was not engaged by athletics, so I would take her on "dad and daughter" dates. We would dress up, and I would take her out to dinner. Once a year our date was to pick out her back-to-school clothing. We would go to department stores and check out the fully accessorized outfits on mannequins. When we found what we liked, I would say to the department clerk, "Give us everything on the mannequin!" We would purchase it all—the little hat, the purse, the shoes, the stockings, the jewelry, the sweater. If I did this as an imperfect dad on a tight budget, how much more the love that the heavenly Father has lavished on us!

Jesus came down to earth to empower us with all the rights, blessings, and responsibilities of what it means to be God's children and to transform us from a fear-based life to a confident, love-filled life. When we haul our manger scene up from the basement each year to decorate for Christmas, or when we hang our children's and grandchildren's stockings from the mantel, it should serve as a reminder that we have been kissed. We were asleep, and then we were kissed. God loves us and has a plan for our lives.

TURNING BACK

Most people in the U.S. believe in God in some form. It's challenging to find many committed atheists in our day-to-day encounters. Believing in God is not the issue for most people; what's difficult is believing that God believes in us. We doubt that we are worthy of God's love.

In Luke 15, Jesus tells a parable about this mistaken perception. A man (representing God in the story) has two sons. The younger son feels he cannot please his father, so he decides to disconnect, move away, and keep a physical and emotional distance. Some of us who have maintained a long-distance relationship with our own parents can relate. Periodically we might phone them out of a sense of obligation, sometimes struggling to get our nerve up before calling. If our parents are more tech-savvy, we may resort to a texting relationship. Communicating becomes a chore to be dreaded instead of a conversation to cherish. In a similar way, many of us have moved away from God and at best have a long-distance relationship. We believe in God, we think about God, we may even talk to God at times, but we always have this sense of unease or discomfort.

In the parable, as in life, when critical relationships break down we often seek substitutes. In Luke 15:12, "the younger one said to his father, 'Father, give me my share of the estate.'" In other words, the son is saying, "We don't have a relationship, Dad, so just send me a check." The younger son gets his part of the estate, pulls together his belongings and cash, sets off for a distant country, and manages to squander his wealth in wild living.

Like the younger son, we too look for substitutes when things with God don't seem to be panning out. Deep down, we desire intimacy with the God who made us, but since we believe that we don't measure up to God's expectations, we go out into the world independent of that relationship and try to define success on our own terms. We begin to pursue the "what" instead of the "who." We believe in God and may try to maintain some type of long-distance relationship, but most of the time we don't pay much attention to God. We may call every once in a while and say, "God, I'm doing pretty well on my own, but could you help me out with this promotion?" or "My baby's sick; could you help her?" or "God, just keep sending me your blessings." We don't have an intimate relationship with the Father, so we seek the Father's things instead of the Father himself.

In Luke 15:17, we see a turn in the younger son's story as we read these words: "When he came to his senses..." Maybe you've experienced that kind of turn. There comes a time when you've received what you thought you wanted. You're doing well at work, you're making more money than you ever thought you could, you married the man or woman you wanted, you have the kids, you have the three-car garage, but you are still empty inside. You are starving relationally, emotionally, and spiritually. You finally realize that a long-distance relationship with God is not sustaining you.

The younger son in the parable turns around and starts making his way back to his father. Luke 15:20 describes what happens next: "But while he was still a long way off, his father saw him and was filled with compassion for him; he ran to his son, threw his arms around him and kissed him." By the way, don't make the mistake of assuming that at this point in the story, the younger son has already managed to put his life back together. The son is still messed up. He may be living with a woman he's not married to; he could be struggling with an eating disorder; perhaps he's in the throes of some unhealthy addiction. No doubt the rank odor of the pigs he had been slopping just days before still clings to his hair and clothes. But the father runs to meet him anyway. Sometimes, like the younger son, we falsely convince ourselves that God is disgusted with us because we are disgusted with ourselves. But God runs to meet us.

Sometimes we falsely convince ourselves that God is disgusted with us because we are disgusted with ourselves. But God runs to meet us.

This is what the Christmas story is all about: God pursuing us! When I think of my shortcomings and brokenness, it's hard to imagine that God looks at me with the same excitement that the parable's father demonstrates for his returning son. But all I need to do is turn back toward the Father. When I do, the Father says, "Quick! Bring the best robe and put it on him. Put a ring on his finger and sandals on his feet" (Luke 15:22).

The parable of the prodigal son depicts the three elements that allow us to return to God: repent, believe, and receive. Some religious people claim that to *repent* means to break all your bad habits and completely overhaul your life so that you can become worthy of God. When viewed in that light, repentance feels horribly negative and in fact impossible. In reality, the word means simply to turn and start walking toward God. That's all. We don't have to change all that's wrong with us; we simply have to turn toward God. In fact, we don't have the power to change ourselves even if we want to. God the Father, who gave his Son for us, is the One who has everything we need.

After repenting, we must *believe* in God's love for us. We may forget God, but our down-to-earth God never forgets us. Finally, we must not only believe God's love but *receive* it. That's because the gift of God's love and forgiveness can never be earned, just accepted. All you can do is unwrap it. You may feel unworthy, but Jesus says, "Who cares? I AM."

BEING LOVED. DOING LOVE.

Once we truly believe ourselves to be loved, we are positioned and ready to do love for others, extending God's love, mercy, and grace to those around us. This year as we approach Christmas, the world seems to be experiencing so little of God's great gifts. Our politics are mean-spirited, our gods are consumerist idols, and new terrorist attacks almost weekly shake our security and our resolve to love others as we love ourselves.

For children of God, horrible acts of evil create all kinds of questions. Why did this happen? How can a loving God allow innocents to be murdered? How do we as people who claim to love God resist the impulse to respond with violence, retribution, or prejudice when evil attacks us through human agents?

If we are to deal with these questions, we need to understand the nature of the real enemy. Our fight is not against people, as the Apostle Paul reminds us:

> For our struggle is not against flesh and blood, but against the rulers, against the authorities, against the powers of this dark world and against the spiritual forces of evil in the heavenly realms. (Ephesians 6:12)

We are in a spiritual war zone, battling a spirit that has as its sole purpose the destruction of people. That spirit is working not only through those who attack us but, subtly, through us as well when we seek retribution.

We become most vulnerable to evil when we are spiritually complacent. General Omar Bradley wrote several decades ago, "Ours is a world of nuclear giants and ethical infants. We know more about war than we know about peace; more about killing than we know about living. We have grasped the mystery of the atom and have rejected the Sermon on the Mount."[4]

Let's point the finger where the blame partly belongs: at us, God's church, when we water down the call of Jesus Christ to be radical agents of love in the world.

Evil has had its play since Cain murdered his brother, Abel. It has slithered and hissed its way through the millennia with little formidable opposition. But there was a cosmic operation being planned under the code name Lion of Judah. Supreme commander over its execution was Jesus of Nazareth, Prince of Peace. In the early morning hours approximately two thousand years ago in a Middle Eastern community called Bethlehem, the armies of heaven invaded Planet Earth and established beachhead communities of light.

The true light has now come "down to earth," and darkness can never put it out.

Lord Jesus, this Christmas help me to grasp the breadth and length and height and depth of your love for me. Then empower me to extend that same all-encompassing, down-to-earth love and compassion into the world that you so loved. Your kingdom come, your will be done. Amen.

Reflection: Can You See the Light?

The true light that gives light to everyone was coming into the world.

(John 1:9)

Sometimes Christmas Eve seems to be filled with anything but light. Some of us have parties to attend, others have family obligations, still others need to stay up half the night assembling Christmas toys. And let's not forget making sure the milk and cookies are prepped and we've put out the reindeer food!

Even for us church professionals, the night before Christmas can seem like a marathon, often with multiple services and celebrations. At times it becomes an evening to endure rather than a celebration to enjoy.

And yet, there's something holy about celebrating Christmas Eve at church. Perhaps it's the warmth of families gathering, or how loud the congregation sings, or the new faces you don't see at other times during the year.

Whatever it is, each Christmas Eve celebration is alive with anticipation.

Sometimes we preacher types think it matters what clever thing we can say about the birth of Jesus. Most of the time I remind our team, and myself, "Let's make sure we simply tell the story."

But no matter how moving the message or powerful the music, here are the real essentials of Christmas Eve: we'd better sing "Silent Night," and we'd better light some candles.

What's up with the candles? Is there a secret pyromaniac dwelling inside each of us? I believe the real passion for lighting candles on Christmas Eve comes in the proclamation that is today's Scripture: "The true light that gives light to everyone was coming into the world." Standing in the darkened sanctuary, we realize the impact of one light, then two, three, four, and so many more. Suddenly, seeing the place light up, the spreading of the gospel, God's good news, makes perfect sense. This story, our story, is contagious! The light is shared, along with the warmth within us. We are part of God's evolving story.

Christmas is a story of hope. When we gather for Christmas celebrations, that hope is clearly proclaimed when each man, woman, and child lights a small wand of wax. Of course, it's not the church tradition that is holy, but the way the candles make Christ's message clear, simple, and tangible for even the youngest person in the room. Lighting the candles answers God's question, "Can you see my light?"

Not every person celebrates the night before Christmas in a church, but I believe all of us have the opportunity to see the light. This Advent season, as you prepare to celebrate Christmas Eve at home or at church, take the time to read the story, light a candle (or several), and proclaim the promise: God's light has come down to earth, where it shines in us and through us.

Light of the World, come, pour out your light and love over us. May we share your light with all we encounter until the whole world has been touched by your love. Lord Jesus, thank you for simple traditions that make tangible the hope you bring in our lives. In your name. Amen.

From *Down to Earth: Devotions for the Season*
by Rachel Billups. Abingdon Press, 2016.

Notes

Notes

Chapter 1

1 Sarah Whitten, "Starbucks Holiday Red Cup Brews Up Controversy On Social Media," *CNBC.com*, November 13, 2015, accessed June 6, 2016, http://www.cnbc.com /2015/11/09/starbucks-holiday-red-cup-brews -controversy-on-social-media.html.

2 Lydia Saad, "Americans Plan on Spending a Lot More This Christmas," *Gallup*, November 16, 2015, accessed June 6, 2016, http://www.gallup.com/poll/186620 /americans-plan-spending-lot christmas.aspx?g_source =Christmas%202015&g_medium=search&g _campaign=tiles.

3 Alexander Roberts and James Donaldson, ed., *The Writings of Tertullian, Vol. 1.*, Vol. 11 of 24 Ante-Nicene Christian Library: *Translations of the Writings of the Fathers Down to A.D. 325* (Edinburgh: T. & T. Clark, 1869), 119.

Chapter 2

1 Alessandro Speciale, "Vatican Defends Pope Francis' Washing Of Women's Feet," *The Huffington Post*, March 30, 2013, accessed June 8, 2016, http://www.huffingtonpost .com/2013/03/30/vatican-defends-pope-francis-washing -of-womens-feet_n_2985784.html.

2   *Strong's Concordance*, s.v. "morphe," accessed June 8, 2016, http://biblehub.com/greek/3444.htm.

3   Richard Rohr, *The Naked Now: Learning to See as the Mystics See* (New York: Crossroad Publishing, 2009), 90.

4   James F. Strange, "Nazareth," in *The Anchor Bible Dictionary*, *Vol. 4*, ed. David Noel Freedman (New York: Doubleday, 1992), 1050–1051.

5   Richard A. Bailey, Waterman, et al., *Preliminary Report*: "Galilee," 7-18; Meyers et al., "Melron," 1-24; Tsuk, "Aqueducts, Sepphoris, 4-19.

6   Haeyoun Park , "Children at the Border, " *The New York Times*, October 21, 2014, accessed June 8, 2016, http://www.nytimes.com/interactive/2014/07/15/us /questions-about-the-border-kids.html?_r=0.

7   C. S. Lewis, *Mere Christianity* (New York: HarperOne, 1952, 1980), 121-122.

8   Thomas Merton, *Disputed Questions* (New York: Farrar, Straus, and Giroux, 1976), Kindle edition.

9   Vivian Yee, "Pope Francis' Popularity Bridges Great Divides," *The New York Times*, Sept. 23, 2015, accessed June 8, 2016, http://www.nytimes.com/2015/09/24/us /pope-francis-popularity-bridges-great-divides.html.

10 Lily Karlin, "Bill Maher Thinks GOP Should Listen To Pope Francis On Climate Change," *The Huffington Post*, September 27, 2015, accessed June 8, 2016, http://www.huffingtonpost.com/entry/bill-maher-pope -francis_us_5606d279e4b0af3706dc7f41.

11   *Christmas Is Not Your Birthday* (Abingdon Press, 2011) and
      the Advent study based on it, *A Different Kind of Christmas*
      (Abingdon Press, 2012), by Mike Slaughter.

12   Dickson Beattie "Doc" Hendley, *Wine to Water: How One
      Man Saved Himself While Trying to Save the World*, (New
      York: Avery Press, 2012), 27.

Chapter 3

1   Dietrich Bonhoeffer, *The Cost of Discipleship* (New York:
     Touchstone, 1995), 44.

2   Gregory Bresiger, "Unused gift cards total $44B since
     2008: study," *New York Post*, January 26, 2014, accessed
     June 9, 2016, http://nypost.com/2014/01/26/unused-gift
     -cards-total-44b-since-2008-study/.

3   "UNHCR warns of dangerous new era in worldwide
     displacement as report shows almost 60 million people
     forced to flee their homes," The UN Refugee Agency
     press release, June 18, 2015, accessed June 9, 2016,
     http://www.unhcr.org/55813f0e6.html.

4   Ibid.

5   "About Sister Dorothy Stang," *Sisters of Notre Dame de
     Namur*, accessed June 9, 2016, http://www.sndohio.org
     /sister-dorothy/.

6   Adapted from Mike Slaughter, *A Different Kind of
     Christmas: Devotions for the Season* (Nashville: Abingdon
     Press, 2012), 49-50.

Chapter 4

1   Carolyn Gregoire, "American Teens Are More Stressed Than Adults," *The Huffington Post*, February 11, 2014, accessed June 9, 2016, http://www.huffingtonpost .com/2014/02/11/american-teens-are-even-m_n _4768204.html.

2   Ann Voskamp, *One Thousand Gifts: A Dare to Live Fully Right Where You Are*, (Grand Rapids: Zondervan, 2010), 59.

Epilogue

1   Jill P. Weber, "4 Ways Social Media Can Undermine Girls and Women," *The Huffington Post*, September, 17, 2014, accessed June10, 2016, http://www.huffingtonpost.com /jill-p-weber-phd-/four-ways-social-media-ca_b_5830540 .html.

2   Douglas Quenqua, "Muscular Body Image Lures Boys Into Gym, and Obsession," *The New York Times*, November 19, 2012, accessed June 10, 2016, http://www.nytimes .com/2012/11/19/health/teenage-boys-worried-about -body-image-take-risks.html?pagewanted=all&_r=1.

3   Alice G. Walton, "New Study Links Facebook to Depression: But Now We Actually Understand Why," *Forbes*, April 8, 2015, accessed June 10, 2016, http://www .forbes.com/sites/alicegwalton/2015/04/08/new-study -links-facebook-to-depression-but-now-we-actually -understand-why/#5e3202112e65.

4   Quoted in Leonard E. Reed, "Nuclear Giants and Ethical Infants," *Foundation for Economic Education*, August 1, 1964, accessed June 10, 2016, http://fee.org/articles/nuclear -giants-and-ethical-infants/.

Acknowledgments

We cannot express thanks enough to our longtime partner The United Methodist Committee on Relief (UMCOR) for its indefatigable work on behalf of those lacking food, safe water, health, and hope in Sudan and South Sudan—and many points beyond. In particular, we are grateful for the support, commitment, and partnership of Thomas Kemper, the current General Secretary of The United Methodist General Board of Global Ministries, and Denise Honeycutt, head of UMCOR. These folk—and those who work with them—have made many of Ginghamsburg Church's "down to earth" miracles possible.

We are also grateful to UMCOR, The United Methodist Publishing House, and United Methodist Communications for their "on mission" partnership with Ginghamsburg on "Beyond Bethlehem," the Christmas Miracle Offering initiative that is assisting refugees in this ever-expanding global crisis.

Of course, thank you also to the faithful Jesus-following servants of Ginghamsburg Church. Without you, we would have far fewer God stories to tell.

Our appreciation to Karen Perry Smith from the Ginghamsburg Church staff team for her assistance in compiling the *Down to Earth* manuscript.

Finally, we save our biggest thank you for Mike's wife, Carolyn, and Rachel's husband, Jon, for their lifelong partnership and encouragement in ministry—and for their patience when we bury our heads in writing projects.

Mike and Rachel

About the Authors

Mike Slaughter, lead pastor at Ginghamsburg Church, is in his fourth decade as the chief dreamer of Ginghamsburg Church and the spiritual entrepreneur of ministry marketplace innovations. Mike's call to afflict the comfortable and comfort the afflicted challenges Jesus followers to wrestle with God and their God-destinies. As both a speaker and an author, Mike is a catalyst for change in the global church. He is the author of many books, including *The Passionate Church, The Christian Wallet, Dare to Dream, Renegade Gospel, shiny gods, Christmas Is Not Your Birthday, Change the World, Spiritual Entrepreneurs*, and *Momentum for Life*.

Rachel Billups serves as Ginghamsburg's executive pastor of discipleship and as part of the preaching team. Before joining the Ginghamsburg team in July 2014, she served as the lead pastor of Shiloh United Methodist, a multisite church in Cincinnati, Ohio. Rachel, an ordained elder within The United Methodist Church, holds a Bachelor's Degree in Bible/Religion and History from Anderson University and a Master of Divinity degree from Duke Divinity School. Rachel was the first clergy resident for the United Methodist West Ohio Conference's Residency Program. She is a coauthor of *Sent: Delivering the Gift of Hope at Christmas*.

Hope for Refugees This Christmas

Global Refugee/Migration Crisis Advance #3022144

A partnership with Ginghamsburg Church, The United Methodist Committee on Relief, The United Methodist Publishing House, and United Methodist Communications.

Awareness is important, but alone not enough. Sacrificial and urgent action is required. We are challenging you this Christmas not to idly stand by as more lives are lost and displaced. Spend only half as much on your own Christmas this year, and give the other half as a Christmas Miracle Offering toward serving the 60 million faces of the refugees Christ loves.

– Mike Slaughter

One in every 122 human beings is now either a refugee, internally displaced, or seeking asylum on Planet Earth.

Millions of refugees are fleeing war, persecution, and violence in their homelands—often running with just the clothes on their backs. Other migrants are escaping from untenable situations of hardship and poverty in their home countries.

The goals of the Global Refugee/Migration Crisis Advance are:

1. **Right to Stay**. Support partner churches, organizations, and communities that are providing alternative possibilities for survival, directly in relation to the communities that are fleeing.

2. **Safe Passage**. Provide protection and access to communication, as well as food, water, and shelter along the traveled routes.
3. **Welcoming and Belonging**. Provide emergency assistance to communities overwhelmed by an influx of refugees and migrants, and provide support for welcoming and integrating the newcomers.
4. **Support for the Returned**. Provide assistance and support to those who have been returned or deported to their countries of origin, so that they may reintegrate with dignity.

For more information about the initiative or to donate, visit: **www.UMCMission.org/Give-to-Mission/Search-for-Projects /Projects/3022144**